silly books
to read aloud

silly books
to read
aloud

ROB REID

an imprint of the American Library Association

HURON STREET PRESS

CHICAGO • 2013

ROB REID, aka Rappin' Rob, has entertained children and their families as a children's humorist and storyteller for more than thirty years. His lively, participative shows feature storytelling, music activities, and wordplay. He is the author of more than a dozen books on children's library programming, including *What's Black and White and Reid All Over? Something Hilarious Happened at the Library* (American Library Association, 2012), as well as two picture books, *Comin' Down to Storytime* (Upstart, 2009) and *Wave Goodbye* (Lee and Low, 1996). In between writing, performing, and teaching at the University of Wisconsin–Eau Claire, Rob writes columns on children's literature for *LibrarySparks* and *Book Links* magazine (a *Booklist* publication) and conducts workshops across North America, entertaining audiences with activities that make literature come alive for children.

Printed in the United States of America
17 16 15 14 13   5 4 3 2 1

Extensive effort has gone into ensuring the reliability of the information in this book; however, the publisher makes no warranty, express or implied, with respect to the material contained herein.

ISBNs: 978-1-937589-10-3 (paper); 978-1-937589-17-2 (PDF); 978-1-937589-18-9 (ePub); 978-1-937589-19-6 (Kindle).

Library of Congress Cataloging-in-Publication Data

Reid, Rob.
    Silly books to read aloud / Rob Reid.
      pages cm
    Includes bibliographical references and index.
    ISBN 978-1-937589-10-3 (pbk.)
      1. Wit and humor, Juvenile—Bibliography. 2. Children's stories—Bibliography. 3. Humorous stories—Bibliography. 4. Children's poetry—Bibliography. 5. Humorous poetry—Bibliography. 6. Picture books for children—Bibliography. 7. Graphic novels—Juvenile literature—Bibliography. I. Title.
    Z6514.W5R45 2013
    [PN1009.A1] 2/13
    011.62—dc23 J LIB
      REI   2012021523

Cover design by Casey Bayer. Cover image © Diego Cervo/Shutterstock, Inc. Text design in Din and Minion Pro, with illustrations courtesy Khrobostova/Shutterstock.

♾ This paper meets the requirements of ANSI/NISO Z39.48-1992 (Permanence of Paper).

For Wesley

Contents

Introduction

Read like a wolf eats.
> —Gary Paulsen

I HAVE FOND memories of reading aloud to my four children. These memories are incredibly important to me. We plowed through *Roll of Thunder, Hear My Cry* by Mildred Taylor, *Shiloh* by Phyllis Reynolds Naylor, the Chronicles of Narnia series by C. S. Lewis, *Charlotte's Web* by E. B. White (with Dad sniffling at the end), and *Where the Red Fern Grows* by Wilson Rawls (with Dad crying outright at the end), to name just a few.

I have a particularly strong memory of reading the fourth Harry Potter book (*Harry Potter and the Goblet of Fire*) to my son Sam when he was ten years old. We had been reading a few chapters every night for a few weeks. One night, around 9 p.m., after reading for an hour and with a few hundred pages left in the book, we reached a point in the story where the two of us looked at each other and knew we were going to finish it that night (luckily there was no school the next morning). We kept going, losing ourselves in the world of Hogwarts. I finished reading at midnight. My voice was gone. We had started on the couch but somewhere along the line had moved to the floor. I read the last word, and, with our heads butting up against the bottom of a rocking chair, we both quietly said, "Whoa." That memory is burned into my brain.

I have other wonderful memories of reading picture books with Sam and his older sisters—Laura, Julia, and Alice—before him. Some favorites were *Many Moons* by James Thurber, *Sylvester and the Magic Pebble* by William Steig, *The Clown of God* by Tomie DePaola, *Millions of Cats* by Wanda Gág, *A Story, a Story* by Gail Haley, *The Relatives Came* by Cynthia Rylant, and dozens of Berenstain Bears books.

The silly books, however, had a special place in our family. We read funny chapter books: *Matilda* by Roald Dahl, the Ramona series by Beverly Cleary, the McBroom books by Sid Fleischman, and *Winnie the Pooh* by A. A. Milne. We read funny picture books, such as *Miss Nelson Is Missing!* by Harry Allard, *The Wolf's Chicken Stew* by Keiko Kasza, *Moira's Birthday* by Robert Munsch, and all of those hilarious books by Dr. Seuss. And not only his picture books, but his easy readers, too, like *Green Eggs and Ham*. We even read silly poetry by Shel Silverstein and Judith Viorst.

I went on to read hilarious books to other people's children. In my roles as a middle school English teacher and as a children's librarian, I had a constant flow of built-in audiences of preschoolers, elementary school children, and middle school students for decades. And humor won them over every time. I read them picture books like the ones I shared with my own children. When my kids got older, I still got to read picture books with my new audiences. We read funny works by Eric Kimmel, Jon Scieszka, Jules Feiffer, and Kevin Henkes. I read them passages from the Junie B. Jones books by Barbara Park as well as Lois Lowry's Sam series. Today, I still get to visit schools and libraries and share newer humor authors, like Doreen Cronin and Mo Willems. I also read these gems to my college students, who are our future teachers, librarians, and parents. And now I have the pleasure of starting all over again with my grandchildren.

A Parent's Guide to the Benefits of Sharing Humor with Children

I think it's important for parents and educators to read aloud to children of all ages. There is a general misconception that when children have learned to read, adults should stop reading to them. Jim Trelease, in his wonderful book *The Read-Aloud Handbook* (6th ed., Penguin, 2006), offers page after page of evidence on the benefits of reading to children of all ages and thus improving the likelihood that they will become lifelong readers. Trelease goes on to show how this helps our society and our country. I like to emphasize that reading aloud to children of all ages makes lifelong readers, lifelong *library users*, and lifelong *learners*.

In this guide, you will find descriptions of some of my favorite humorous children's books currently in print and available for purchase at major bookstores. Availability was one of my criteria for including a book in this guide. Some of the companion books listed with these titles may be out of print but, in this age of online used bookstores, it shouldn't be too hard to find these, too. The books are organized by format: picture books, easy readers, chapter books (fiction), poetry collections, and graphic novels and manga (a Japanese graphic novel style that is very popular with American kids).

Picture books work well with preschoolers and primary grade students (K–2). Many picture books contain several layers of humor and thus appeal to a larger audience. Often lines are aimed at adults, such as famous movie lines like "You had me at hello" and "Here's looking at you, kid," in the picture book *Rescue Bunnies* by Doreen Cronin. Easy readers for the most part are written with controlled vocabularies and are designed to help children learn to read on their own. This doesn't mean adults shouldn't read them aloud. While many easy readers are clunky to read aloud, the titles in this guide are all fun read-alouds. Adults sometimes forget poetry when it comes to reading aloud with children. I frequently have college students tell me that their young reading partner doesn't like any of the books they're sharing. The first thing I ask is, "Have you tried poetry?" (The second thing I ask is, "Have you tried nonfiction?" which isn't the focus of this guide but is something for parents to consider.) I direct these students to the works of Shel Silverstein, Judith Viorst, Douglas Florian, Jack Prelutsky, and Adam Rex. Finally, how, or even why, should adults read graphic novels and manga to kids? One reason is that they are extremely popular today. Kids will learn to associate graphic novels with reading, and then they will associate reading with fun. Take the time to read each dialogue balloon and each sound effect that appears along with the main text, and I guarantee a good shared read-aloud experience.

Find a quiet place to read to your child or children. Make sure the television, radio, and stereo are off in that area. Many families choose the children's bedroom right before the lights go out as a good time and location. Don't use the threat of not reading aloud as a punishment. Try to avoid creating negative connotations with the joy of reading aloud. I recommend using your normal speaking voice with a hint of "elusive awe." In other words, a quiet excitement and wonder should be reflected in your voice as you and your child enter the world of the book. Some folks like to have different voices for different characters, some don't. Choose what feels right for you. When reading humor, in particular, I like to be expressive and then throw in a subtle facial expression, like lifting an eyebrow when something weird happens in the story, or making an oval shape with my mouth when something surprising happens. These little things help my listeners know that I am just as excited about the story as they are.

Please note, too, that humor is very subjective. Not every type of humor is for everyone. A certain sort of humor might make one person uncomfortable, while another person is crying with laughter. Some of the books in this guide use sophisticated wordplay. Some titles contain potty humor. Some titles have both. In writing the annotations, I did my best to give a taste of what kind of humor each book in this guide employs, without being too much of a watchdog. So find the books that work for you and have a silly time with your young ones.

The Library as a Resource Partner

This guide recommends more than 180 humorous books to read aloud to children. Few folks have the budget to buy this many books.

The library is one of the greatest inventions in the world (up there with the car and the iPod and the snowblower . . .). Many public libraries will have the lion's share of the titles in this book. Libraries that can't afford to buy all the titles they want often participate with other libraries to provide interlibrary loan services. Take advantage of these services—they're a wonderful use of your taxes. Many libraries also have a "Suggestion for Purchase" service. If there's a book in this guide you want to look at and your library doesn't have it, ask them to buy it for their collection. Get to know your librarian. Wonderful new humor titles are released each year. Librarians are trained to keep abreast of these titles, and many of them love to share this knowledge with their patrons. You yourself can check out free sources like the *New York Times* best-seller lists that are posted online each week. Your library may subscribe to review periodicals like *Booklist* or children's resource magazines like *LibrarySparks*. If they don't make these resources available to the public, ask your librarian if you can look over some recent issues to locate new silly children's books.

Enough of the introduction! Plunge into the descriptions of the wonderful books on the following pages, make your lists, grab the books, and start reading!

The Silliest Picture Books

Agee, Jon
Milo's Hat Trick
Illustrated by the author. Hyperion, 2001

Milo the Magnificent is not a very good magician. "He botched his card trick. He tangled his rope trick. And his hat trick was pathetic." He is told to pull a rabbit out of his hat or else. Instead of a rabbit, Milo catches a bear. The bear is very adept at hiding in a hat. He agrees to help Milo with his show, but the two become separated. The bear finally locates Milo, and the magician becomes a success. "After popping in and out of seven hundred and sixty-two hats," the bear decides to quit the show. Milo lets him go and learns how to dive into the hat himself. The illustration of the bear popping out of the hat in a crowded restaurant going "TA-DA!" is precious.

Alexander, Lloyd
The Fortune-Tellers
Illustrated by Trina Schart Hyman. Dutton, 1992

A young carpenter is unhappy with his work. He wonders what the future holds for him. He finds a fortune-teller in the neighboring town. The fortune-teller's first prediction is "You're going to pay me a nice fee." He also tells the young man that he'll become rich: "On one condition: that you earn large sums of money." The carpenter enjoys this prediction as well as others. He leaves, but then realizes he has more questions. When he goes back, the fortune-teller is no longer there. A woman mistakes the carpenter for the fortune-teller. "You've changed yourself into a handsome young man!" The carpenter starts playing the role of the fortune-teller. He becomes successful. When a customer

Milo's Hat Trick by Jon Agee

asks if she will live a long life, the new fortune-teller responds, "Indeed so. You only need to stay healthy and keep breathing." We later see a humorous, multipage explanation of the disappearance of the first fortune-teller.

Allard, Harry
Miss Nelson Is Missing!
Illustrated by James Marshall. Houghton Mifflin, 1977

"The kids in Room 207 were misbehaving again." They are the worst-behaved students in the whole school. "They were even rude during story hour." They finally drive their nice teacher, Miss Nelson, away. The kids are forced to shape up when confronted by the meanest substitute in the world—Viola Swamp. Viola has a cruel-looking face, wears an ugly black dress, and has a no-nonsense attitude. The students start looking for Miss Nelson. They even go to the police. Miss Nelson returns and the kids are ecstatic. "Miss Nelson noticed that during story hour no one was rude or silly." Later on in the book, we see an ugly black dress in Miss Nelson's closet.

Companion books: *Miss Nelson Is Back* (Houghton Mifflin, 1982); *Miss Nelson Has a Field Day* (Houghton Mifflin, 1985)

Alley, Zoë B.
There's a Wolf at the Door: Five Classic Tales
Illustrated by R. W. Alley. Roaring Brook, 2008

A wolf moves from one story to another in this collection of five traditional folktales. First he encounters the three pigs—Alan, Gordon, and Blake—and runs away from them when he fails to get into the brick house. The wolf also appears in versions of "Little Red Riding Hood," "The Wolf and the Seven Little Goslings," "The Wolf in Sheep's Clothing," and "The Boy Who Cried Wolf." In this last story, the sheep make hilarious asides about the young shepherd, such as "What a mutton head," and "We all had such high hopes for him. Better than Little Bo Peep."

Arnold, Tedd
Catalina Magdalena Hoopensteiner Wallendiner Hogan Logan Bogan Was Her Name
Illustrated by the author. Scholastic, 2004

This book is based on an old nonsensical camp song. We see Catalina Magdalena grow up and notice that there are some peculiar things about her. "Well, she had two peculiar hairs on her head; One was black and one was red . . . some folks say her breath smells sweet; But me, I'd rather smell her feet." She also has two holes in her nose—"one for her fingers and one for her toes." Catalina Magdalena eventually graduates from high school, gets a job at a fish factory, falls in love, and marries a man named Smith. Arnold includes other variations of her name in the back matter along with a score of the song.

Aylesworth, Jim
The Completed Hickory Dickory Dock
Illustrated by Eileen Christelow. Atheneum, 1990
We learn what happens after the famous nursery rhyme is over and the clock strikes two. "Nibble on, bibble on, bees. / The mouse bit off some cheese. / The clock struck two, / Away he flew. / Nibble on, bibble on, bees." When the clock strikes three, the mouse scratches a flea. When the clock strikes four, the mouse rolls on the floor (while wearing a cape and mask). After the cat chases the mouse into a hole, the clock strikes five and the mouse is happy to be alive. The mouse plays some tricks on the cat when the clock strikes six. The rhyme continues through the mouse having wonderful dreams. "The clock struck twelve, / Now dream some yourselves. / Silvery, bilvery, beams."

Aylesworth, Jim
The Tale of Tricky Fox: A New England Trickster Tale
Illustrated by Barbara McClintock. Scholastic, 2001
Tricky Fox develops a plan to trick a human out of a fat pig. His brother says he'll eat his hat if the plan works. Tricky Fox finds an elderly woman. He asks her to watch his sack but not to look into it. The woman looks into the sack anyway and finds only a log. When she falls asleep, the fox throws the log into the fire. The next morning, he looks in his sack and wonders what has happened to his loaf of bread. The woman can't tell him there was no bread without giving up the fact that she peeked into the sack. So she gives him a loaf of bread. The fox pulls a similar trick with another old woman. On his third attempt, the lady places her bulldog in Fox's sack. Tricky Fox missed one important thing—the third lady was a teacher. "And Tricky Fox didn't know that teachers are not so easy to fool as regular humans are."

Bachelet, Gilles
My Cat, the Silliest Cat in the World
Illustrated by the author. Abrams, 2006
The narrator talks about his cat, including how he sleeps on the couch but has little bursts of energy during which he runs around the house. The illustrations show that the "cat" is really an elephant. Young readers will enjoy the scenes of the elephant hiding in the washing machine, cleaning itself (sucking water from the toilet with his truck and spraying itself), and using the litter box. The narrator mentions that cats usually land on their feet after falling and concedes that his cat doesn't (we see the elephant on its back with a broken loft railing overhead). The book ends with the narrator unsuccessfully trying to figure out his cat's breed from a cat book.
  Companion book: *When the Silliest Cat Was Small* (Abrams, 2007)

Bar-el, Dan
Such a Prince
Illustrated by John Manders. Clarion, 2007

This retelling of the folktale "The Three Peaches" is narrated by Gaborchik the fairy. "As fairies go, I'm not the flashy kind. Glass slippers and pumpkin carriages are just not my style." She helps Marvin, the youngest of three sons, win the hand of the princess, who is "deathly ill." Marvin brings three peaches to the princess, and she "jumps to her feet, and begins to dance a fandango." The king tries to keep Marvin from marrying his daughter by giving him seemingly impossible tasks. During one of his tasks, Marvin tricks the king into kissing a donkey three times. When the donkey-kissing incident is about to be revealed, his majesty interrupts: "Test's over." The king insists that Marvin and the princess get married immediately.

Barnett, Mac
Guess Again!
Illustrated by Adam Rex. Simon & Schuster, 2009

What looks like a simple rhyming guessing game for little children turns into a series of fun and absurd setups. For example, the first illustration shows a silhouette of what looks like a bunny. The text reads, "He steals carrots from the neighbor's yard. / His hair is soft, his teeth are hard. / His floppy ears are long and funny. / Can you guess who? That's right! My . . ." We anticipate the answer will be bunny. However, when we turn the page, we find that the answer is instead "Grandpa Ned." No, his name doesn't rhyme, but his contortions correctly match the silhouette. Grandpa Ned shows up again, and when we finally anticipate "Ned," because the setup rhyme is "bread," the answer turns out to be "Grandpa Alan."

Barrett, Judi
Animals Should Definitely Not Wear Clothing
Illustrated by Ron Barrett. Atheneum, 1970

If animals wore clothing, there'd be all sorts of problems. The hilarious illustrations depict a porcupine's quills poking through the clothes, a goat eating its outfit, a sheep getting too hot, a mouse completely covered by its hat, a camel wearing hats on its humps, and a walrus getting its clothes all wet. It would also be unnecessary for a kangaroo (we see the kangaroo wearing a coat with big pockets) and silly for a giraffe (it's wearing several neckties on its long neck). The funniest picture is that of a hen wearing pants and hovering near its nest. There is a silhouette of an egg in the bottom of the pants, unable to drop down into the nest. The book concludes with a picture of an elephant wearing the same floral-patterned dress as a woman.

Companion book: *Animals Should Definitely Not Act like People* (Atheneum, 1980)

Barrett, Judi
Cloudy with a Chance of Meatballs
Illustrated by Ron Barrett. Atheneum, 1978
A man tells his grandchildren "the best tall-tale bedtime story he'd ever told." "There were no food stores in the town of Chewandswallow." That's because food fell from the sky, three times a day—breakfast, lunch, and dinner. Folks would watch the weather forecast on the television to see what the menu of the day would be. "After a brief shower of orange juice, low clouds of sunny-side up eggs moved in followed by pieces of toast." It also rained soup and juice and snowed mashed potatoes and green peas. Hot dogs blew in, and when the winds shifted, baked beans fell. One day, the weather took a turn for the worse. The headlines of the paper read "Spaghetti Ties Up Town!" Kids were upset because they had Brussels sprouts for their birthday parties. The townspeople left Chewandswallow on rafts made from giant peanut butter sandwiches and sailed to a new land where food could only be found in stores.

Companion book: *Pickles to Pittsburgh* (Atheneum, 1997)

Barton, Chris
Shark vs. Train
Illustrated by Tom Lichtenheld. Little, Brown, 2010
A shark and an anthropomorphic train compete head-to-head in many silly situations. Sometimes a scenario gives the advantage to the shark and sometimes it gives the advantage to the train. The train has the advantage at an amusement park. There is a long line of kids waiting to ride the train. No one is in line to go on the shark ride. In fact, there is a sign that reads, "You Must Be This Crazy to Go on This Ride," complete with a height indicator. The shark has the advantage when jumping off the high dive into a pool of water. In the end, we see two boys playing with a toy shark and a toy train.

Birdseye, Tom
Soap! Soap! Don't Forget the Soap!
An Appalachian Folktale
Illustrated by Andrew Glass. Holiday House, 1993
Plug has a poor memory. His mother sends him on an errand to buy soap. She tells him, "'Now don't forget, Plug,' she said with the faith that only a mother could have. 'Soap! Soap! Don't forget the soap!'" He chants this phrase over and over. He startles a woman, who falls into a creek. She dunks him and says, "What a mess I've become, but now you're one, too!" Plug continues on his trip, but now he says this new phrase. He repeats it when he sees a boy who has fallen off his bike. The boy thinks Plug is making fun of him and tosses Plug in the blackberry brambles. The boy says, "Look who's in a fix now!" Of course, Plug says this new phrase until he comes across another person. Eventually, someone mentions the word "soap," and Plug remembers his task. His mother looks at her now messy boy, tells him, "I'd say soap is just what we need," and plunks him in a wooden bathtub.

Bluemle, Elizabeth
My Father, the Dog

Illustrated by Randy Cecil. Candlewick, 2006

A child has a theory that her father is really a dog. "Consider the evidence." Indeed, the father is shown next to the family dog in each illustration, almost mimicking the pet. Father starts the day by scratching himself, fetching the newspaper, chasing a ball, and investigating noises. He also likes to roughhouse, lie around for hours, and ride in the car with the windows rolled down. He will growl "when you startle him out of a nap." He is very loyal to the entire family, which is good, because "Mom says we can keep him." All ages will be particularly amused by the fact that "when he toots, he looks around the room like someone else did it."

Bottner, Barbara
Miss Brooks Loves Books! (and I Don't)

Illustrated by Michael Emberley. Knopf, 2010

Miss Brooks, the school librarian, is super-excited about books. She dresses up as children's book characters and "all year long . . . reads us books." Some of the characters Miss Brooks dresses up as are the Runaway Bunny, Babar the elephant, one of the wild things from *Where the Wild Things Are*, and the caterpillar from *The Very Hungry Caterpillar*. Unfortunately, the narrator doesn't feel the same way about books. She asks her mother if they can move. "My mother says there's a librarian in every town." The girl finally gets excited when she finds the book *Shrek* by William Steig. She dresses up as "a stubborn, smelly, snorty ogre."

Brown, Peter
Children Make Terrible Pets

Illustrated by the author. Little, Brown, 2010

Lucy, a young bear, finds a human boy in the woods. It squeaks at her. "OH! MY! GOSH! You are the cutest critter in the WHOLE forest!" She brings the boy to her mother and asks if she can keep him. Her mother replies, "Children make terrible pets." Lucy convinces her mother, and she and the boy play together, eat together, and nap together. There are problems. The boy ruins the furniture, refuses to use the litter box, and throws temper tantrums. Lucy is devastated when the boy goes missing. She follows his scent through the woods and sees that he's reunited with his human family (to Lucy's ears, they are all squeaking, too).

Bruchac, Joseph, and James Bruchac
How Chipmunk Got His Stripes: A Tale of Bragging and Teasing

Illustrated by Jose Aruego and Ariane Dewey. Dial, 2001

Bear brags about being the biggest, strongest, and loudest animal of them all. Brown Squirrel challenges Bear by asking Bear to tell the sun not to rise in the morning. Bear shouts, "SUN, DO NOT COME UP TOMORROW." Bear and Brown Squirrel stay up all night. Bear sings, "The sun will not come up, humph!" Brown Squirrel starts singing, "The sun is going to rise, oooh!" When the sun comes up, Bear is very grumpy. Brown Squirrel foolishly teases Bear. "WHOMP! Bear's big paw came down on Brown Squirrel, pinning him to the ground." Brown Squirrel tricks Bear into lifting up his paw just enough so he "could take a deep breath and apologize." Brown Squirrel escapes, but Bear's claws rake his back, leaving white scars. And that's why we now have Chipmunk. To this day, Chipmunk still sings his morning song, and Bear is the last animal to wake up, because he dislikes Chipmunk's song.

Companion books: *Turtle's Race with Beaver: A Traditional Seneca Story* (Dial, 2003); *Raccoon's Last Race: A Traditional Abenaki Story* (Dial, 2004)

Bruel, Nick
Bad Kitty
Illustrated by the author. Roaring Brook, 2005

This ABC book goes through the alphabet not once, not twice, but four times. The first time through, we see Bruel's trademark cat being offered healthy food from Asparagus to Zucchini. Bad Kitty is not happy and decides to be bad. She misbehaves her way through the alphabet, from "Ate My Homework" to "Zeroed the Zinnias." Kitty leaves a nasty note when she quarrels with the neighbors. The note reads, "Dear Neighbor, Meow Hiss Hiss Hiss Meow Meow Hiss Meow!" Bad Kitty is then offered a weird litany of food, from "An Assortment of Anchovies" to "Zebra Ziti." Bad Kitty decides to be good and alphabetically atones for her naughtiness, from "Apologized to Grandma" (for biting her earlier) to lulling the baby to sleep, "Zzzzzzzz."

Companion books: *Poor Puppy* (Roaring Brook, 2007); *A Bad Kitty Christmas* (Roaring Brook, 2011). There are also chapter books featuring Bad Kitty.

Bryan, Sean
A Boy and His Bunny
Illustrated by Tom Murphy. Arcade, 2005

A boy wakes up to find a bunny on his head. He names the bunny Fred. "'Good morning,' said Fred, the bunny on his head. And the boy got out of bed with you-know-who on his head." The two go about their day. His mother is puzzled at the sight of her son, but the boy tells her, "You can do anything with a bunny on your head." Examples include spreading peanut butter, leading armies, and exploring the seabed. His mother tells him that he looks cool with a bunny on his head. At that moment, the boy's sister walks in with an alligator on her head.

Companion books: *A Girl and Her Gator* (Arcade, 2006); *A Bear and His Boy* (Arcade, 2007)

Calmenson, Stephanie
The Principal's New Clothes
Illustrated by Denise Brunkus. Scholastic, 1989

Principal Bundy is the sharpest dresser in town in this retelling of "The Emperor's New Clothes." His students call out, "Looking good, Mr. B!" Sometimes Mr. Bundy goes home at lunch and changes, "just to show off." A couple of tricksters named Moe and Ivy ask Mr. Bundy if he'd "like to buy an amazing, one-of-a-kind suit." They inform him that the suit is made from special cloth that's "invisible to anyone who is no good at his job or just plain stupid." Mr. Bundy pays for his new suit. He plans to premiere it at the school assembly. "That night Mr. Bundy had cold and drafty dreams." When Mr. Bundy walks into the auditorium, a kindergartner yells, "The principal's in his underwear!" Mr. Bundy is embarrassed, but the students and teachers help out by passing up parts of their own clothing. The last picture shows Mr. Bundy wearing this mish-mash of clothes with the caption "Mr. Bundy was still the sharpest dresser in town."

Companion book: *The Frog Principal* (Scholastic, 2001)

Catalanotto, Peter
Matthew A.B.C.
Illustrated by the author. Atheneum, 2002

This is my all-time favorite alphabet book, because the different Matthews represented sometimes border on the absurd. Mrs. Tuttle has twenty-five children in her class (all boys—can you imagine?), and they are all named Matthew. Each Matthew has a character trait that begins with a different letter of the alphabet. Matthew A is extremely affectionate and can be seen constantly hugging his teacher. Matthew B has Band-Aids all over his body. Matthew C has cowlicks that spell out words. Adult readers will be particularly amused by some of the Matthews' outrageous traits, such as Matthew F, who has a cat on his face, and Matthew J, who works a night job (and is seen napping in grease-stained overalls with rags and wrenches in his pockets). Of course, the class gets a new Matthew at the end of the book—Matthew Z with all of his zippers.

Child, Lauren
I Will Never Not Ever Eat a Tomato
Illustrated by the author. Candlewick, 2000

Lola is a fussy eater. She has a long list of food she won't eat, "and I absolutely will never not ever eat a tomato." Lola's brother Charlie tricks her into eating healthy food. He gives each food item a new name and identity. He pulls out some carrots and Lola immediately declares, "I don't ever eat carrots." He tells her they aren't carrots; they are orange twiglets from Jupiter. She tries one. "'Mmm, not bad,' she said, and took another bite." Peas become green drops from Greenland, mashed potatoes are cloud fluffs from Mount Fuji, fish sticks are ocean nibbles, and the dreaded tomatoes are moonsquirters. Ask your child to come up with new names for common foods.

There are more than a dozen Charlie and Lola books. The second in the series is *I Am Not Sleepy and I Will Not Go to Bed* (Candlewick, 2001).

Child, Lauren
That Pesky Rat
Illustrated by the author. Candlewick, 2002

A city rat is friends with a variety of domestic pets. The rat learns about the advantages of being someone's pet: sitting on a feather cushion, hanging out, or doing puzzles with one's owner. The pets also inform the rat about the downsides of being a pet. These include taking baths, being bored when one's owner is away, or dressing up in a hat and coat. "But I would do anything to be somebody's pet," says the rat. He puts up a poster that says, "Brown rat looking for kindly owner with an interest in cheese." A local pet store owner helps out. Soon, the nearsighted Mr. Fortesque comes in and takes the rat, mistaking it for a *cat*. Neither the rat nor the pet store owner corrects him.

Christelow, Eileen
Five Little Monkeys Jumping on the Bed
Illustrated by the author. Clarion, 1989

This picture book is based on the popular fingerplay. "It was bedtime. So five little monkeys took a bath." They also put on their pajamas, brush their teeth, and say good night to their mother. "Then . . . five little monkeys jumped on the bed!" The first monkey falls off, and the upset mother calls the doctor. She puts an ice pack on his head. The second monkey falls off and gets a bandage wrap. An increasingly frustrated doctor monkey repeats the key phrase, "No more monkeys jumping on the bed!" One by one, the monkeys fall off the bed. Once the five injured monkeys go to sleep, we see Mama monkey jumping on the bed.

Companion books: *Five Little Monkeys Sitting in a Tree* (Clarion, 1991); *Don't Wake Up Mama! Another Five Little Monkeys Story* (Clarion, 1992); *Five Little Monkeys with Nothing to Do* (Clarion, 1996); *Five Little Monkeys Wash the Car* (Clarion, 2000); *Five Little Monkeys Play Hide-and-Seek* (Clarion, 2004); *Five Little Monkeys Bake a Birthday Cake* (Clarion, 2004); *Five Little Monkeys Go Shopping* (Clarion, 2007); *Five Little Monkeys Reading in Bed* (Clarion, 2011)

Cole, Brock
Buttons
Illustrated by the author. Farrar Straus Giroux, 2000

When an old man's buttons pop off his britches, his three daughters work to solve the problem. The eldest daughter decides to walk around until a rich man falls in love with her and asks for her hand in marriage. She plans to say, "No!

I can never be yours! Not unless you first give me all of your buttons!" The second daughter joins the army disguised as a boy so she can wear a soldier's uniform, which has several buttons. "I shall be able to spare two or three for Father." The youngest daughter plans to run around outside, holding her apron to catch buttons as they fall out of the sky. Of course, things don't go as planned, but in the end, all three daughters get married and Father gets his buttons.

Cole, Brock
The Money We'll Save
Illustrated by the author. Farrar Straus Giroux, 2011

Pa goes off to the market to buy two eggs and half a pound of flour, but he comes home with a young turkey. "It will fatten up into a fine bird, and we can have it for Christmas dinner. Think of the money we'll save!" They name the turkey Alfred. The neighbors complain, especially Mrs. Schumacher, who comes upstairs three times a day. "Once to complain about the noise, once to complain about the smell, and once to complain about her back and feet and how hard it was for a woman her age to climb up and down all those stairs three times a day." The day before Christmas, Pa tells the family that their worries are over and he'll prepare the bird. The family is horrified at the thought of eating Alfred. "They decided to give Alfred to Mrs. Schumacher as a Christmas present." (She is pleased because the turkey reminds her of the late Mr. Schumacher.)

Collins, Ross
Dear Vampa
Illustrated by the author. HarperCollins, 2009

A family of vampires, drawn in black and white, are dismayed by their new neighbors, drawn in full color, who appear to be normal humans. When the vampires try to sleep during the day, the new neighbors—the Wolfsons—are making noise. The vampires are disgusted by the fact that the Wolfsons lie out in the sun. The new neighbor children don't seem to warm up to the vampires' pet, Cuddles (a large creature with tentacles). The funniest scene is when the vampire father is drinking what he thinks is a glass of blood. He spits it out when he realizes it is tomato juice. The vampires pack up their things and go to stay with Vampa in Transylvania.

Cox, Judy
Don't Be Silly, Mrs. Millie!
Illustrated by Joe Mathieu. Marshall Cavendish, 2005

A young teacher makes her class laugh with her silly announcements. She tells the students to hang up their goats, instead of their coats (the illustrations show several goats hanging by their horns in the cloakroom). Mrs. Millie also tells the children to get out their paper and penguins (pens), not to cut in lion (line) to get a drink, and to wash their hands with soap and walrus (water). Before recess, she warns them to not step in a poodle (puddle), and at the end of recess, she calls for them to "chameleon" (come in). At the end of the school day, she has them put on their bats and kittens (hats and mittens) to get ready to go home. The children come back with their own Millie-ism: "We wave good-bye as we get on the octopus" (bus).

Companion books: *Mrs. Millie Goes to Philly!* (Marshall Cavendish, 2008); *Pick a Pumpkin, Mrs. Millie!* (Marshall Cavendish, 2009); *Happy Birthday, Mrs. Millie!* (Marshall Cavendish, 2012)

Creech, Sharon
A Fine, Fine School
Illustrated by Harry Bliss. HarperCollins, 2001

Principal Keene loves his students, his teachers, and, most of all, his school. He decides to extend school to Saturdays. He then adds Sundays. He also has school on the holidays. No one knows how to tell him that they don't want to go to school this much. It's not until he has everyone attend in the summer that young Tillie lets him know that they need a break now and then. The illustrations are a hoot. Take a look at Tillie's dog, Beans, whenever he appears. In one scene, Beans is wearing a baseball catcher's gear. Also keep an eye out for the written jokes illustrator Bliss has scattered around. There's a banner in the school cafeteria that reads, "Why Not Study While You Chew?" One child is holding a book titled "This Book Is Way Too Hard for You," while a classmate's backpack has written on it, "How's my walking? 1-800-SAF-WALK."

Cronin, Doreen
Diary of a Worm
Illustrated by Harry Bliss. HarperCollins, 2003

A young worm sporting a red baseball cap discusses the advantages and disadvantages of being a worm. Some of the negative aspects include not being able to chew gum or keep a pet dog. On the positive side, worms never get into trouble for tracking mud into the house. And they never have to go to the dentist. "No cavities—no teeth, either." Worm makes his friend Spider fall out of a tree from laughing too hard (Worm is shown wearing an arrow-through-his-head prop). Worm and his friends dance to "The Hokey Pokey." They put their heads in and their heads out. "You do the hokey pokey and you turn yourself about. That's all we could do." A few pages later, Worm teases his sister by telling her that her "face will always look like her rear end."

Companion books: *Diary of a Spider* (HarperCollins, 2005); *Diary of a Fly* (HarperCollins, 2007)

Cronin, Doreen
Dooby Dooby Moo
Illustrated by Betsy Lewin. Atheneum, 2006

Dooby Dooby Moo finds Farmer Brown's animals entering a talent show. The cows sing "Twinkle, Twinkle, Little Star," and the sheep sing "Home on the

Range." The pigs are supposed to do an interpretive dance, but when they fall asleep, Duck fills in with his rendition of "Born to Be Wild." Adults will appreciate the legalese Cronin, a lawyer herself, sprinkles throughout the book. For example, the talent show ad states that the first prize, a trampoline, is in used condition and has no warranty. The description of the second-prize item, a box of chalk, comes with a note: "Actual amount awarded will be based on availability." Third prize is a Veggie Chop-O-Matic.

Companion books: *Click, Clack, Moo: Cows That Type* (Simon & Schuster, 2000); *Giggle, Giggle, Quack* (Simon & Schuster, 2002); *Duck for President* (Simon & Schuster, 2004); *Click, Clack, Quackity-Quack: An Alphabetical Adventure* (Atheneum, 2005); *Click, Clack, Splish, Splash: A Counting Adventure* (Atheneum, 2006); *Thump, Quack, Moo: A Whacky Adventure* (Atheneum, 2008). There are also board books featuring these farm animals.

Cronin, Doreen
Rescue Bunnies
Illustrated by Scott Menchin. HarperCollins, 2010

Newbie is a beginner first responder. She and her shift pick up a distress signal. A young giraffe is stuck in mud, and a pack of hyenas is on the horizon. When the rest of her crew threatens to pull out before the hyenas arrive, Newbie leads everyone to make one final effort to free the poor giraffe. The text is full of classic movie lines. For example, one of the crew tells Newbie, "You can't handle the truth." Newbie reassures the young giraffe that "nothing is going to hurt you tonight. Not on my watch." The giraffe replies, "You had me at hello." At the end of the story, the Chief tells Newbie, "Here's looking at you, kid." Cronin even sneaks in the corny bit where one bunny tells another, "Surely you can't be serious," and the second bunny replies, "Don't call me Shirley."

Cuyler, Margery
That's Good! That's Bad!
Illustrated by David Catrow. Holt, 1991

The author uses the traditional joke story game to tell a tale about a young boy who is separated from his family at the zoo. His parents give him a balloon. "Oh, that's good. No, that's bad!" The balloon carries him to the jungle. The balloon pops on the branch of a prickly tree. "That's bad! No, that's good!" The boy breaks his fall by landing in a river near some hippos and climbs up on one. "Oh, that's good. No, that's bad." The boy is chased by some baboons. His adventure continues in this vein. The boy encounters a snake, a giraffe, an elephant, and a lion. When he finally cries, his tears create a puddle that attracts a thirsty stork. The stork delivers the boy back to his parents. "Oh, that's good. No, that's GREAT!"

Companion books: *That's Good! That's Bad! in the Grand Canyon* (Holt, 2002); *That's Good! That's Bad! in Washington, D.C.* (Holt, 2007); *That's Good! That's Bad! on Santa's Journey* (Holt, 2009)

Deacon, Alexis
A Place to Call Home
Illustrated by Viviane Schwarz. Candlewick, 2011

When their home (a hole in a mattress in the dump) gets too small for them, seven hamsters venture out into the world to find a new home. They don an assortment of junk (rubber gloves, a teacup, a lampshade, a paper towel tube, a boot, a faucet) to make ready for their quest. They cross a sea (a puddle) and a desert (what looks to be salt spilled from a bag) and reach the end of the world (they're standing on top of a washing machine). When the junkyard dog makes off with one of the hamsters, the others bravely grab the "beast" (one has its tail, one has its ear, and another has "something"—the dog's chain). They put the various items of junk on the dog (which makes for one hilarious illustration) and find their new home—the outside world. "This place looks nice."

Demas, Corinne
Always in Trouble
Illustrated by Noah Z. Jones. Scholastic, 2009

Toby the dog is in trouble every day. For example, on Monday, he gets into the garbage. On Tuesday, he runs into the road. On Wednesday, he eats an entire loaf of bread. On Thursday, he barks in the middle of the night. On Friday, he wets the rug. On Saturday, he chews up "all the buttons on Emma's new coat." On Sunday, he snoozes, and on Monday, he gets into the garbage again. His owner, Emma, takes him to dog training school. He is the perfect student. However, once back home, he causes trouble again. He goes back to school to become "a specially trained dog." When he returns home this time, he takes out the garbage on Monday. He is *almost* a perfect dog. There is a surprise on the last page of the book—a torn hole! Apparently caused by Toby.

Denim, Sue
The Dumb Bunnies
Illustrated by Dav Pilkey. Blue Sky, 1994

This rabbit version of "Goldilocks and the Three Bears" features a cast of not-too-bright bunny characters. They live in a log cabin made out of bricks. The parents' porridge is too hot and too cold, but Baby Bunny's is just right. So he pours it down his pants. The bunnies leave the house and go ice-skating at the bottom of a lake, go bowling at the library (one of the books on display is *Green Eggs and Tofu*), and have a picnic in the car wash. While they are gone, Little Red Goldilocks breaks into their house. The bunnies return and flush her down the toilet. Look at the various signs scattered throughout; one announces a "Speling Bee." A sticker on the book's cover announces: "This book is TOO DUMB to win an award." Dav Pilkey used a "pseudonym" as the author of this work ("a Sue Denim").

Companion books: *The Dumb Bunnies' Easter* (Blue Sky, 1995); *Make Way for Dumb Bunnies* (Blue Sky, 1996); *The Dumb Bunnies Go to the Zoo* (Blue Sky, 1997)

DePaola, Tomie
Fin M'Coul: The Giant of Knockmany Hill
Illustrated by the author. Holiday House, 1981

Fin M'Coul, the giant, is afraid of Cucullin, an even bigger giant. Folks say of Cucullin, "when he walked, the very earth trembled, and with one blow of his fist he had flattened a thunderbolt so it looked like a pancake." In fact, Cucullin walks around with the flattened thunderbolt in his pocket to impress everyone. Fin's wife, Oonagh, cleverly dresses Fin up as a baby and passes him off as his own son. Fin looks pretty ridiculous sitting in a gigantic cradle with a baby bonnet on his head. But the trick works. Cucullin worries that the strength of the baby son of Fin M'Coul means that the father is even stronger.

Duffield, Katy S.
Farmer McPeepers and His Missing Milk Cows
Illustrated by Steve Gray. Rising Moon, 2003

Nearsighted Farmer McPeepers loses his glasses (the cows take them). He looks out the window the next morning and says, "Good heavens! Where are my milk cows?" He goes looking for them. He passes by some fishermen on Meyer's Pond (the fishermen are cows), youngsters swimming (more cows), children playing on the town's playground (cows), and so on. We even see a line of moviegoers (again, his cows) waiting to see "Cowabunga Summer Starring Surf Legend Duke Kahana Moocow." Farmer McPeepers stumbles across his glasses and, once he puts them on, is surprised to find himself surrounded by his cows.

Elya, Susan Middleton
Oh No, Gotta Go!
Illustrated by G. Brian Karas. Putnam, 2003

A little girl is in the car with Papá and Mamá when she says, "Where is un baño? ¿Dónde está?" The family frantically races around town looking for a bathroom. "Hurry, Papá. ¡Más rápidamente!" They finally enter a blue "restaurante," only to find a long line of people waiting to get into the bathroom. The other ladies give the girl and her mother permission to go ahead of them. "I went to the baño, came out with a sigh, and thanked the nice ladies who let me go by." The family eats and drinks (the little girl has a huge glass of "limonada") and heads home. Of course, a few minutes into their drive, the girl asks, "Where is un baño? ¿Dónde está?"

Companion book: *Oh No, Gotta Go #2* (Putnam, 2007)

Ernst, Lisa Campbell
Goldilocks Returns
Illustrated by the author. Simon & Schuster, 2000

Years after the original story, Goldilocks (now an old woman) is feeling guilty about her horrid behavior as a young girl. She goes to the bears' house to "set things right!" The bears are older, too. In fact, the young one, "though not a baby for some fifty years now, still went by the name Baby Bear." While they are out on a walk, waiting for their porridge to cool (some things never change), Goldilocks installs new locks on their door, replaces their porridge with Rutabaga Breakfast Bars and Tart-n-Tasty Celery Juice, and restores Baby Bear's broken chair (changing it into a rocking horse). The bears find Goldilocks sleeping on their bed. She wakes up, gives them a hug, and leaves in her truck. The bears are upset at the changes she made.

Ernst, Lisa Campbell
Walter's Tail
Illustrated by the author. Bradbury, 1992

Mrs. Tully gets a new puppy and names him Walter. His tail never stops wagging. Everyone in town thinks it's cute. However, when Walter grows, "*that* was when the trouble began." His tail knocks over Mrs. Tully's jigsaw puzzle—"the one with 2,768 pieces." Mrs. Tully tells him that everyone makes mistakes. "Calamity struck on their daily trip to town." Walter knocks the fruit displays down at the grocer's. He knocks down nails at the hardware store. And when the two visit the candy shop, "a barrel of lemon balls tumbled, turning the floor into a lemon-ball sea." Mrs. Tully decides they are too wild for town, and they walk up a hill. The townspeople notice how quiet it is and begin to worry about Mrs. Tully and Walter. Mrs. Tully gets her foot stuck in a crevice on the hill. Walter's wild tail signals the folks down in town to their location. Afterward, everyone talks about how cute Walter's tail is.

Falconer, Ian
Olivia
Illustrated by the author. Atheneum, 2000

Olivia is a lively little pig who "is *very* good at wearing people out. She even wears herself out." She dresses up, sings "40 Very Loud Songs," sees a Jackson Pollack painting at the museum and tries to duplicate it on a wall in her family's home, and builds, not a sand castle, but a sand skyscraper. At the end of the day, she negotiates with her mother about the number of bedtime books to be read. This book has my all-time favorite line in any children's picture book: When Olivia's mother tells her daughter, "You know, you really wear me out. But I love you anyway," Olivia responds with, "I love you anyway too."

Companion books: *Olivia Saves the Circus* (Atheneum, 2001); *Olivia . . . and the Missing Toy* (Atheneum, 2003); *Olivia Forms a Band* (Atheneum, 2006); *Olivia Helps with Christmas* (Atheneum, 2007); *Olivia Goes to Venice* (Atheneum,

The vet reached deep down inside of George . . .

And pulled out a cat.

Bark, George by Jules Feiffer

2010). Olivia also appears in board books and books adapted from the television series.

Feiffer, Jules
Bark, George
Illustrated by the author. HarperCollins, 1999

George's mother tells her puppy to bark. Instead, George meows. "No, George. Cats go meow. Dogs go arf. Now, bark, George." George quacks, oinks, and moos. George's mother takes him to the vet. "'I'll get to the bottom of this,' said the vet." The vet reaches down George's throat and pulls out a cat, a duck, and a pig. "Then he reached deep, deep, deep, deep, deep, deep, deep, deep, deep, deep, deep down inside of George . . . and pulled out a cow." George is then able to bark. The mother kisses the vet (as well as the cat, the duck, the pig, and the cow). When George's mother takes him out for a walk among people in the streets, she asks him to bark. George says, "Hello."

Feiffer, Jules
I Lost My Bear
Illustrated by the author. Morrow, 1998

A young girl loses her teddy bear and drives her family crazy. Her sister instructs her to close her eyes and throw one of her other stuffed animals. "Sometimes it lands in the same place." The girl has trouble choosing which stuffed animal to toss. She does "eeny meeny miny mo" and points to her stuffed bunny rabbit. She hollers that her bunny rabbit is her second favorite stuffed animal after her teddy bear. "Goodbye! Goodbye! Goodbye! Goodbye! Goodbye! I can't do it!" Her sister finally lends her a stuffed animal to toss. In the end, of course, the teddy bear turns up in the girl's bed. The little girl's hysterics are fun to read aloud. "I c-c-c-could-could-couldn't finnnnnnd her because yoooouuuuuuuu would-would-wouldn't hellllllllp meeeeeeeeee!"

Fleming, Candace
Muncha! Muncha! Muncha!
Illustrated by G. Brian Karas. Atheneum, 2002

Mr. McGreely is proud of his new garden. Unfortunately, three rabbits "Tippy-Tippy-Tippy, Pat" into Mr. McGreely's garden and eat the produce. He builds a wire fence. The rabbits hop over it. He builds a tall wooden wall. The rabbits burrow under it. Mr. McGreely digs a moatlike trench. The rabbits still get to the garden with a "Spring-Hurdle, Dash" and a "Dig-Scrabble, Scratch," and a "Dive-Paddle, Splash." Next, Mr. McGreely builds what looks like a prison around the garden, complete with searchlights, wire, and padlocks. The rabbits can't get in. Mr. McGreely is happy. He enters the garden with a basket to gather the vegetables. The rabbits hop out of the basket and start eating. In the end, we see Mr. McGreely sharing his food with the rabbits.

Companion book: *Tippy-Tippy-Tippy, Hide!* (Atheneum, 2007)

Friedman, Laurie
I'm Not Afraid of This Haunted House
Illustrated by Teresa Murfin. Carolrhoda, 2005

A young boy bravely leads his small group of friends into a haunted house, where they encounter a scary cast of characters, from a witch to a one-eyed monster. He brags, "I'm Simon Lester Henry Strauss, and I'm not afraid of this haunted house." He boldly bares his neck in front of a vampire and directs a bloody werewolf to the nearest bathtub. He joins the monsters for a meal of blood and brains and guts and veins. The final pages build up the tension as Simon crawls into a coffin, sticks a toe into a pool of blood, walks through a pitch-black room, and balances on a moving floor. His friends have the final laugh when Simon loudly proclaims, "I'M NOT AFRAID OF THIS . . . EEEEEEEEEEEEEEK . . . A MOUSE!"

Gerstein, Mordicai
A Book
Illustrated by the author. Roaring Brook, 2009

A little girl and her family live inside a book. When the book is opened, they wake up. We see them eat breakfast before Father goes off to be a clown, Mother fights fires, and Brother grows up to be an astronaut. The little girl worries. "Everyone has a story but me. What's *my* story?" Several literary characters with funny word balloons attempt to help the girl. A witch tells her, "Taste my roof! Taste my door! You can even eat my floor!" Her cat says, "This is a historical novel and I love it! It's full of mice!" In a particularly fun scene, a goose is telling the little girl about readers. The girl asks, "What are . . . readers?" The goose tells her to look up. The girl sees us and cries "EEEEEK! What's that huge . . . *blobby* thing that looks something like a face?" The girl eventually decides to become an author.

Goble, Paul
Iktomi and the Boulder
Illustrated by the author. Orchard, 1988

Iktomi is a vain trickster. As he is walking to a neighboring village, he thinks, "How handsome I look . . . Everyone will be impressed. All the girls will want me to notice them." He gets hot during his journey and places his blanket on top of a boulder. He then notices rain clouds and takes back the blanket. The boulder chases Iktomi, rolls on his legs, and traps him. None of the animals can push the boulder off Iktomi. That evening, he tells the bats that the boulder was making fun of them. "He said that you sleep upside-down because you don't know your 'up side' from your 'down side.'" The bats break off pieces of the boulder until there is "nothing left but little chips." Iktomi walks on, not looking like such a dandy after all. This Plains Indian folktale "also explains why bats have flattened faces and why there are rocks scattered all over the Great Plains."

Companion books: *Iktomi and the Berries* (Orchard, 1989); *Iktomi and the Ducks* (Orchard, 1990); *Iktomi and the Buffalo Skull* (Orchard, 1991); *Iktomi and the Buzzard* (Orchard, 1994); *Iktomi and the Coyote* (Orchard, 1998); *Iktomi Loses His Eyes* (Orchard, 1999)

Graves, Keith
Chicken Big
Illustrated by the author. Chronicle, 2010

A humongous chick is born to a very small hen. An acorn falls on a small chicken who worries the sky is falling. The big chick calms the other chickens down by eating the acorn. The same thing happens the next day with a drop of rain. Again, the big chick stops the panic. Every time the big chick helps out, the other chickens guess he must be something other than a chicken: "Apparently, he is an umbrella." When the smallest chicken blurts out that the big chick must be an elephant, the narrator informs us, "She was not the sharpest beak in the flock." A fox steals several eggs and the big chick once again saves the day. (The fox believes the big chick is a hippopotamus.)

Grossman, Bill
My Little Sister Hugged an Ape
Illustrated by Kevin Hawkes. Knopf, 2004
The narrator's goofy sister is on a hugging spree and goes after an alphabetical array of animals. When she squeezes the ape, it lets out a burp. After she hugs a tiny bug, it flies up her nose. And when she hugs a cow, it squirts milk all over. One of the more comical hugs comes with the letter R. Sister hugs a rat. It goes flat, so she blows in its ear to reinflate it so she can hug it again. When Sister hugs the zebra, the stripes aren't dry and Sister wears them instead. In the end, the little sister is "hugging ME!"

Companion book: *My Little Sister Ate One Hare* (Crown, 1996)

Henkes, Kevin
Julius, the Baby of the World
Illustrated by the author. Greenwillow, 1990
Lilly is jealous of her new baby brother. "I am the queen. And I hate Julius." When no one is looking, she insults him and mixes up the alphabet while he is sleeping in his crib. Lilly has a hard time believing Julius is staying permanently. "After Julius goes away, can I talk like a normal person again?" She even learns magic in hopes that he'll disappear. She tells her original story, "Julius the Germ of the World," to her family. "The story earned her ten minutes in the uncooperative chair." When Cousin Garland visits and calls Julius disgusting, Lilly gets mad. She makes Cousin Garland hold Julius and shout "Julius is the Baby of the World!"

Companion books: *Lilly's Purple Plastic Purse* (Greenwillow, 1996); *Lilly's Big Day* (Greenwillow, 2006)

Himmelman, John
Chickens to the Rescue
Illustrated by the author. Holt, 2006
Farmer Greenstalk loses his watch down the well. More than two dozen chickens show up, wearing a variety of swimming gear. They dive down into the well and retrieve the watch. "'Those are some chickens!' said Farmer Greenstalk." Mrs. Greenstalk is too tired to make dinner. The chickens flock to the kitchen and whip up a meal. The dog eats Jeffrey Greenstalk's homework. The chickens do research on the computer and write a new report for Jeffrey. The duck drives away with the family's truck. The chickens catch up and form a chain

to stop the truck. (One chicken is seen blowing a whistle.) Finally, "a big wind blew Milky the cow into a tree." The chickens create another chain and guide the cow over to a trampoline. The sheep wander off and get lost. The chickens hoist the sheep on their backs and bring them back. When Emily spills her cereal, nobody comes forward to help. We see the chickens sleeping in the hen house.

Companion books: *Pigs to the Rescue* (Holt, 2010); *Cows to the Rescue* (Holt, 2011)

Hong, Lily Toy
Two of Everything
Illustrated by the author. Whitman, 1993

Mr. Haktak and Mrs. Haktak are old and poor. One day while gardening, Mr. Haktak uncovers a brass pot. He takes it home to his wife. "'I wonder what we can do with it,' said Mrs. Haktak. 'It looks too large to cook in and too small to bathe in.'" She accidentally drops a hairpin in the pot and is shocked when she pulls out two hairpins. They also discover that Mr. Haktak had dropped his coin purse in the pot and now there are two of them. Mr. and Mrs. Haktak cannot believe their good fortune. Then Mrs. Haktak falls into the pot, and two Mrs. Haktaks come out. The same thing happens to Mr. Haktak. Afterward, the two sets of Haktaks become very good friends and neighbors. And they are very, very careful what they put into the pot.

Hort, Lenny
The Seals on the Bus
Illustrated by G. Brian Karas. Holt, 2000

When this book came out, I slapped my forehead and said, "Why didn't I think of this?" Readers will have no trouble singing the text to the tune of the traditional song "The Wheels on the Bus." The seals on the bus go "errp, errp, errp," the tiger goes "roar, roar, roar," the geese go "honk, honk, honk," the rabbits go up and down, the monkeys go "eeeeh, eeeeh, eeeeh," the vipers go "hiss, hiss, hiss," and the sheep go "bah, bah, bah." The skunks upset everyone by going "sssss, sssss, sssss," and the people on the bus leave, screaming, "help, help, help!" (At least, the adult humans do. The kids are having a good time.)

Huget, Jennifer LaRue
How to Clean Your Room in 10 Easy Steps
Illustrated by Edward Koren. Schwartz & Wade, 2010

"The first thing we need is a messy room. The messier, the better." The first step to cleaning your room is to wait until it's so messy that your mother hollers using all three of your names. Then pull out everything from your drawers and closets and pile it all in the middle of the room. Sort the items into three piles: "One pile of stuff that's broken. One pile of stuff you're too grown-up to play with anymore. And one pile of things that you love more than anything else in the world." Of course, this last pile is many times larger than the other two piles put together. Put the first two piles into one box and leave it in your sister's room. When your mother tells you to get rid of the one-eyed bunny, cry, "NO! Not Poofball!" After your mother leaves, throw Poofball "back in the heap and forget about her." After sharing many more instructions like these, the young narrator is all set to "show you how to fix your hair."

Isaacs, Anne
Dust Devil
Illustrated by Paul O. Zelinsky. Schwartz & Wade, 2010
Angelica "Angel" Longrider, a larger-than-life modern-day tall-tale character, lives in Montana, "a country so sizeable that even Angel could fit in." She wrestles a dust storm that contains a giant horse—Dust Devil—and creates the Grand Canyon as she holds on for the ride. She encounters Backward Bart and his Flying Desperadoes gang, who ride on giant mosquitoes. "A Montana mosquito can carry a heavy suitcase and two watermelons on each wing without sweating." Angel moves a mountain closer to her cabin to create shade. Her neighbors all want a mountain, too. When Angel sets a new mountain down, she says, "That's a beaut . . . And to this day, every stand-alone peak in Montana is called a butte."

Companion book: *Swamp Angel* (Dutton, 1994)

Jackson, Alison
I Know an Old Lady Who Swallowed a Pie
Illustrated by Judith Byron Schachner. Dutton, 1997
An old lady shows up at the door and swallows a pie. "A Thanksgiving pie, which was really too dry. Perhaps she'll die." The old lady next swallows some cider "that rumbled and mumbled and grumbled inside her" to moisten the pie. Next, she swallows a roll whole, then a squash ("oh my gosh"), followed by a salad, a turkey, a pot, a ten-layer cake, and finally some bread. "'I'M FULL,' SHE SAID." By the end of the book, the old lady has grown so large that they attach ropes to her and fly her as a float at the Thanksgiving parade.

James, Simon
Baby Brains
Illustrated by the author. Candlewick, 2004
"In the months before Baby Brains was born," his parents read to "the baby inside her tummy," play music, and "even turned up the television when the news came on." On his first day home, Mrs. Brains finds her baby reading the newspaper. Mr. Brains finds him fixing the car. Later that evening, "Baby Brains spoke his first words . . . 'I'd like to go to school, tomorrow.'" The infant not only goes to school, but also begins "working as a doctor at the local hospital." Some scientists ask Baby Brains if he'd like to go into outer space. While taking a space walk, the extraordinary baby wails, "I want my mommy!"

Baby Brains goes back to being a baby, but on the weekends "he still likes to help out at the local hospital."

Companion books: *Baby Brains Superstar* (Candlewick, 2005); *Baby Brains and RoboMom* (Candlewick, 2008)

Jarman, Julia
Class Two at the Zoo
Illustrated by Lynne Chapman. Carolrhoda, 2007

Class Two sees many things at the zoo. "They saw a koala kissing a kangaroo" and "a giraffe having a laugh." What they didn't notice was the anaconda. The huge reptile stalks the class and swallows Kyle. And then James and Jake. "They didn't see that twisty beast add Diana to his feast." The teacher and other classmates are also swallowed. Molly grabs a stick, and she and the remaining students open the snake's mouth and pull out their teacher and classmates, as well as "a boy they didn't know." Everyone emerges covered with snake slime. The book ends with the warning that when visiting a zoo, "if you see the anaconda open an eye and start to wander, don't even for a second ponder . . . run!"

Companion book: *Class Three at Sea* (Carolrhoda, 2008)

Jeffers, Oliver
Stuck
Illustrated by the author. Philomel, 2011

Floyd gets his kite stuck high up in a tree. He throws his shoe at the kite to knock it loose, but "that got stuck too!" After throwing his other shoe, he throws a cat named Mitch. "Cats get stuck in trees all the time, but this was getting ridiculous." Floyd continues to throw a variety of things at the kite: a ladder, a bucket of paint, a duck, a chair, a bicycle, the front door, the family car, the milkman, an orangutan, a small boat, a big boat, a rhinoceros, a truck, the house across the street, a lighthouse, "a curious whale, in the wrong place at the wrong time," and, yes, the kitchen sink. "And they all got stuck." Firemen show up to help out. Floyd throws them and the fire engine, too. Finally, Floyd gets a saw—and throws it up. Luckily, it knocks down the kite and Floyd runs off to play with it. Later that night, "he could have sworn there was something he was forgetting."

Jenkins, Emily
That New Animal
Illustrated by Pierre Pratt. Farrar Straus Giroux, 2005

A new baby comes into a home. The two dogs—FudgeFudge and Marshmallow—do not like that "new animal smell." They are jealous because they are no longer the center of attention. The two dogs think about eating the new animal. "'We'd get in trouble,' says Marshmallow. 'Then we'll just bite it.' 'No.' 'Bite it a LITTLE bit?' 'No.'" They think about burying the new animal like a bone and sleeping in the new animal's cradle. Marshmallow pees all over the carpet. However, when Grandpa comes, the dogs are very protective of the new animal and bark at Grandpa to stay away. "It's not *his* new animal to go picking up whenever he feels like it. It's *our* animal."

Johnston, Tony
Bigfoot Cinderrrrrella
Illustrated by James Warhola. Putnam, 1998
"Once upon a time, in the old-growth forest, a band of Bigfoots lived." Among them is a Bigfoot prince. He is so hairy that all of the Bigfoot women want to marry him. They pick flowers, drape them around themselves, and bat their eyelashes when he is near. He, on the other hand, is more interested in nature than them. "'*No pick flowers!*' he bellowed at them." A Bigfoot woman, her two daughters, and her stepdaughter, Rrrrrella, also live in the forest. Rrrrrella has to do all the work. She's not invited to the Bigfoot prince's fun-fest. Her beary godfather transforms her and gives her a new pair of bark-clogs. Rrrrrella does the logroll with the prince and dunks him. Horrified, she runs away and loses her clog. The prince goes looking for his "stinking beauty." Of course, "her foot fit the clog like a seed in a pod," and a rowdy wedding followed.

Kasza, Keiko
Don't Laugh, Joe!
Illustrated by the author. Putnam, 1997
Mother Possum decides that it's time to teach her son, Joe, "the most important lesson a possum can learn"—how to play dead. It's hard for Joe to learn this trick because he constantly giggles. She finally takes him outside and pretends to be a "grumpy old bear." Just then, a real bear runs over and growls. Joe plays dead. The bear sniffs Joe. He pokes Joe's tummy. He shakes Joe up and down. The bear sits and watches Joe, but Joe doesn't move. "Suddenly, the bear started to cry big tears." He only wanted Joe to make him laugh, but instead Joe fell down dead. Joe pops up and reassures the bear that he's OK. Joe makes the bear laugh. The bear thanks Joe for teaching him how to laugh, and Joe thanks the bear "for teaching me how to play dead." At the end of the story, the bear and all of Joe's woodland friends drop to the ground and play dead.

Kasza, Keiko
My Lucky Day
Illustrated by the author. Putnam, 2003
A fox is surprised when a pig appears at his door. The pig seems surprised, too. The fox grabs the pig and a roasting pan. "This must be my lucky day. How often does dinner come knocking on the door?" The pig convinces the fox that he's too dirty to eat. The fox gives the pig a bath. Next, the pig suggests that he's too small to eat. The fox makes the pig a meal of spaghetti and cookies. The pig tells the fox he's too tough to eat. The fox gives the pig a massage. Finally,

the fox collapses from exhaustion. The pig runs away (with the rest of the cookies), looks at his address book (we see that the fox and a coyote have check marks next to their names), and wonders which animal he'll visit next. The last illustration shows the pig "accidentally" appearing on a bear's doorstep.

Kasza, Keiko
The Wolf's Chicken Stew
Illustrated by the author. Putnam, 1987

A wolf gets a terrible craving for some chicken stew. He spots his prospective victim and follows her. He stops short of pouncing on her, thinking, "If there was a way to fatten this bird a little more, there would be all the more stew for me." He runs home and makes "a hundred scrumptious pancakes." He drops them off on the chicken's porch. "The next night he brought a hundred scrumptious doughnuts." On the third night, be drops off a hundred-pound cake. Each evening, the wolf says, "Eat well, my pretty chicken. Get nice and fat for my stew!" When he finally decides to catch the chicken, she surprises him by gathering her baby chicks and exclaiming all the food items were "presents from Uncle Wolf!" The chicks give him one hundred kisses. Naturally, the wolf decides he can no longer eat the chicken. Instead, he decides to bake a hundred cookies.

Keller, Laurie
Arnie the Doughnut
Illustrated by the author. Holt, 2003

Arnie is an excited doughnut. He loves the bakery and is thrilled when a man buys him. However, Arnie is horrified when he learns that the man plans to eat him. Arnie introduces himself and learns that the man's name is Mr. Bing. The two of them come up with lists of things to do with Arnie besides eating him. They decide to let Arnie become a pet doughnut-dog. "Rolling over? Look at me—I was MADE for rolling over!" The little comments by other characters many of them doughnuts—add to the book's humor. One long john prefers to be called "Long Jonathan." A cruller says, "Bonjour, Madame." Arnie flirts with an apple fritter. "Any relation to Larry Fritter?" The customers in the bakery are also amusing. A caveman says, "Doughnuts make good wheel."

Keller, Laurie
The Scrambled States of America Talent Show
Illustrated by the author. Holt, 2008

The state of New York wants to put on a talent show. The other states are excited, except Georgia, who has a case of stage fright. Dr. Globe tells her to "try picturing the audience in their underwear." Uncle Sam helps the states put the show together. Some states work behind the scenes. "Arizona was the costume designer." The other states practice solo and group performances. Minnesota saws South Dakota in half, and North Dakota is in on the trick. Iowa tells corny jokes and Wisconsin makes cheese sculptures. Take time to read the many mini-dialogues throughout the book. During intermission, Vermont tells us, "If you need to use the 'you-know-what,' now would be a good time."

Companion book: *The Scrambled States of America* (Holt, 1998)

Kellogg, Steven
Sally Ann Thunder Ann Whirlwind Crockett
Illustrated by the author. Morrow, 1995

A new infant was born more than two hundred years ago. "'Howdy! I'm Sally Ann Thunder Ann Whirlwind!' shouted the baby in a voice as loud as a blast of buckshot." She brags that she can "out-talk, out-grin, out-scream, out-swim, and out-run any baby in Kentucky!" At the age of one, Sally beats the fastest runner in the state. She flips the strongest arm wrestlers at the age of four, and on her eighth birthday, she sets out to find adventures on the frontier. She invents bald eagles by blasting the color off the heads and tails of regular eagles. She rescues Davy Crockett and decides to freshen up. She "grabbed a hornet's nest for a bonnet and fogged herself with the perfume of passing skunk." The two fall in love and get married. With Davy away serving in the United States Congress, Sally saves the day by defeating a gang of bull alligators.

Companion books: *Paul Bunyan* (Morrow, 1984); *Pecos Bill* (Morrow, 1986); *Johnny Appleseed* (Morrow, 1988); *Mike Fink* (Morrow, 1992)

Kent, Jack
The Caterpillar and the Polliwog
Illustrated by the author. Prentice-Hall, 1982

A snooty caterpillar goes around the pond and brags, "When I grow up, I'm going to turn into something else." One turtle responds, "I don't blame you." A polliwog is excited about the caterpillar's words. A fish informs the polliwog that he, too, will turn into something else. "Fish know things. They go to school." The caterpillar is a bit upset. She thought only caterpillars could do it. When she informs the polliwog that she'll turn into a beautiful butterfly, the polliwog assumes he'll become a butterfly, too. He watches the caterpillar spin a cocoon and disappear out of sight. He fails to notice that, while watching the cocoon, he is turning into a frog. When the butterfly emerges and flies off, the frog is puzzled. "I thought I was going to turn into a butterfly." However, he admires his new self in his reflection, while in the background a new caterpillar brags about turning into something else.

Ketteman, Helen
Armadillo Tattletale
Illustrated by Keith Graves. Scholastic, 2000

Long ago, "Armadillo's ears were as tall as a jackrabbit's and as wide as a steer's horns." He uses his large ears to spy on the other animals. When he overhears Muskrat saying Rattlesnake's rattles used to be out of tune but now sound won-

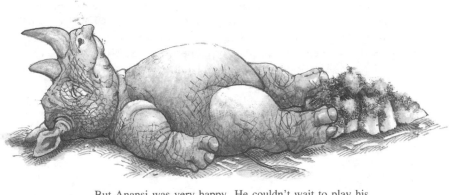

But Anansi was very happy. He couldn't wait to play his trick again. He played it on Rhinoceros

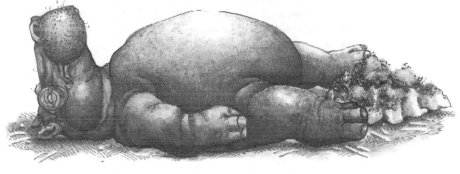

and Hippopotamus.

Anansi and the Moss-Covered Rock by Eric A. Kimmel

derful, Armadillo runs to Rattlesnake and tells him that Muskrat said "your rattles sound terrible and out of tune." Armadillo spreads misinformation to other animals as well. Every time one of the animals gets mad at Armadillo, they throw a hissy fit. "SQUAAAAWK! SQUAAAWK! AAAAWK!" They also peck away at his ears. Today Armadillo has tiny ears, which actually allow him to run faster (he kept tripping over his old ears). He uses speed to his advantage, but no longer overhears what the other animals are saying.

Kimmel, Eric A.
Anansi and the Moss-Covered Rock
Illustrated by Janet Stevens. Holiday House, 1988
Anansi the spider finds a rock with mysterious powers. When someone says "moss-covered rock" in its presence, "KPOM," they faint. Anansi uses this

magic to trick the other animals. He convinces Lion to take a walk with him. Anansi points to the rock. Lion says, "Isn't this a strange moss-covered rock?" and promptly faints. Anansi runs back to Lion's house and steals his yams. Anansi also tricks Elephant, Rhinoceros, Hippopotamus, Giraffe, and Zebra. The pictures of the various large animals lying in dead faints are hilarious. Little Bush Deer overhears Anansi's secret. She uses his trickery against him and then helps the other animals retrieve what belongs to them. Unfortunately, Anansi doesn't learn his lesson and is "still playing tricks to this very day."

Companion books: *Anansi Goes Fishing* (Holiday House, 1992); *Anansi and the Talking Melon* (Holiday House, 1994); *Anansi and the Magic Stick* (Holiday House, 2001); *Anansi's Party Time* (Holiday House, 2008)

Klassen, Jon
I Want My Hat Back
Illustrated by the author. Candlewick, 2011

A bear notices that his hat is gone. He goes looking for it. He asks a fox if he's seen the hat. The fox has not. The bear asks a frog, who hasn't seen it either. He next asks a rabbit wearing a red hat. The rabbit replies, "No. I haven't seen it. I would not steal a hat. Don't ask me any more questions." The bear moves on and asks a few more animals. Suddenly, the bear realizes he has seen his hat recently. He catches up to the rabbit and shouts, "YOU. YOU STOLE MY HAT." The two stare at each other. On the next page, the bear is enjoying his hat. Someone asks the bear if he has seen a hat-wearing rabbit. The bear protests, "No. I haven't seen him. I haven't seen any rabbits anywhere. I would not eat a rabbit. Don't ask me any more questions."

Kloske, Geoffrey
Once upon a Time, the End
Illustrated by Barry Blitt. Atheneum, 2005

A father reads to his child at night. "But as he read, he started cutting little words here and there and the stories would go faster, and faster, and faster." We are treated to shortened versions of such classics as "Chicken Little," "Goldilocks and the Three Bears," "The Little Red Hen," and "Sleeping Beauty." Some of the titles themselves get shortened, such as "The Two Little Pigs." Most stories end with some reference to going to sleep. The story of "Princess Pea" describes the sensitive princess who couldn't sleep because of the pea under the mattress. The father ends the story with, "And so she married the prince. Is there a pea under your bed? Then what's your excuse? Go to bed."

Knutson, Barbara
Love and Roast Chicken:
A Trickster Tale from the Andes Mountains
Illustrated by the author. Carolrhoda, 2004

Cuy, the guinea pig, spots the dangerous fox Tío Antonio. Cuy quickly "squeezed under the edge of a great rock and pressed up with his arms." He convinces Tío

Antonio that he's actually holding up the sky with the rock. Otherwise, the sky would fall on them. "I've been here all day, and I need to go to the bathroom. Please, will you hold the rock for just a moment?" Tío Antonio holds the rock the entire day before realizing he has been tricked. Cuy next traps Tío Antonio in a den, convincing the fox that the world is burning. When a farmer catches Cuy stealing alfalfa, Cuy tricks the fox into taking his place, promising him the love of the farmer's daughter and a plate of the farmer's chickens every day.

Krosoczka, Jarrett J.
Punk Farm
Illustrated by the author. Knopf, 2005
When Farmer Joe goes to the house for the evening, some of his animals get ready to play rock and roll. Pig plays guitar, Cow plays drums, Chicken plays keyboards, Goat plays bass, and Sheep sings lead vocals. The horses wear sunglasses, take tickets, and act as security. Before the concert, the band huddles backstage. "'Are you guys ready?' asks Sheep. 'I was born ready,' says Pig. 'Whatever, dude,' says Goat." The other farm animals pack the barn, and when Sheep hits the stage, he yells, "Who's ready to rock?" The band plays a rousing version of "Old MacDonald." At the end of the concert, Sheep shouts out, "Thank you, Wisconsin!" The next day, Farmer Joe finds all of the farm animals sound asleep.

Companion book: *Punk Farm on Tour* (Knopf, 2007)

LaRochelle, David
The Best Pet of All
Illustrated by Hanako Wakiyama. Dutton, 2004
A boy tries to convince his mother that he should have a dog. She tells him dogs are too messy and loud. Then he asks for a dragon. She's amused and says, "If you can find a dragon, you can keep it for a pet." He finds a dragon at the drugstore and brings it home. The dragon causes many problems, and the mother quickly gets fed up. The boy informs his mother that dragons are afraid of dogs. She agrees that they need a dog. The boy puts up a "Dog Wanted" sign, and within moments a dog appears. At the end of the book, we see the dragon giving the boy a thumbs-up.

LaRochelle, David
The Haunted Hamburger and Other Ghostly Stories
Illustrated by Paul Meisel. Dutton, 2011
Two ghost children named Franny and Frankie ask Father Ghost to tell them a scary story. The first story is called "The Scary Baby" and features a ghost named Uncle Ned who is having trouble scaring humans. An old man tells the ghost that he has a cute costume and gives him a gumdrop. A teenager starts singing a "Boo" song. A baby mistakes Uncle Ned for his blankie. When Ned hollers, the baby starts crying, so Uncle Ned hides in an open drawer. The baby's mother comes in and decides the baby needs a new diaper. She

reaches inside the drawer, and unfortunately for Uncle Ned, he becomes the new diaper. Father Ghost tells the ghost children, "I told you it was a scary story." In addition to the title story, the book includes a story titled "The Big Bad Granny." The scariest thing about her is her kisses.

Lester, Helen
Tacky the Penguin
Illustrated by Lynn Munsinger. Houghton Mifflin, 1988

Tacky the penguin lives on an island with five other penguins—Goodly, Lovely, Angel, Neatly, and Perfect. Tacky is the odd one of the bunch. He slaps the other penguins on the back and yells, "What's happening?" Tacky wears a Hawaiian shirt and makes cannonball dives. He sings strange songs like "How Many Toes Does a Fish Have?" He also marches out of step: "1-2-3, 4-2, 3-6-0, 2½, 0." A group of hunters shows up with plans to catch the penguins and "sell them for a dollar." While the other penguins hide, Tacky marches up to the hunters and slaps them on the back with a hearty, "What's happening?" He marches out of step, sings loudly, and does a splashy cannonball. The hunters are confused by this wild penguin and run away. The other penguins now appreciate having an odd bird around.

Companion books: *Three Cheers for Tacky* (Houghton Mifflin, 1994); *Tacky in Trouble* (Houghton Mifflin, 1998); *Tacky and the Emperor* (Houghton Mifflin, 2000); *Tackylocks and the Three Bears* (Houghton Mifflin, 2002); *Tacky and the Winter Games* (Houghton Mifflin, 2005); *Tacky Goes to Camp* (Houghton Mifflin, 2009); *Tacky's Christmas* (Houghton Mifflin, 2010)

Lester, Julius
Sam and the Tigers
Illustrated by Jerry Pinkney. Dial, 1996

Author Lester and illustrator Pinkney have recreated *The Story of Little Black Sambo*, preserving the fun aspects of the original story while removing several of the stereotypes that were associated with various editions of the book. "Once upon a time there was a place called Sam-sam-sa-mara, where the animals and the people lived and worked together like they didn't know they weren't supposed to." All the people in Sam-sam-sa-mara are named Sam. Young Sam goes with his father Sam and his mother Sam to the marketplace to buy clothes for school. They pick up a red coat at "Mr. Elephant's Elegant Habiliments. (Mr. Elephant liked words as big as him that nobody could say.)" They buy purple pants at Monkey's Magnificent Attire, a yellow shirt at The Feline's Finest Finery, silver shoes at Mr. Giraffe's Genuine Stupendous Footwear Emporium, and a green umbrella from Brer Rabbit. On his way to school, Sam encounters tigers that relieve Sam of his new clothes. The tigers start fighting and turn into a pool of butter. That evening, Sam's family uses the butter on their pancakes. Sam eats one hundred and sixty-nine pancakes. "Wearing all them colors can really make a boy hungry."

Levine, Gail Carson
Betsy Who Cried Wolf
Illustrated by Scott Nash. HarperCollins, 2002

Betsy sets out to be "the best shepherd in Bray Valley history." A wolf named Zimmo has a plan to eat some sheep. While Betsy is keeping a ewe from tumbling into the Soakenwetz River, Zimmo jumps out in plain sight. Betsy blows her wolf whistle, and "every farmer in Bray Valley pounded up to the pasture." Zimmo sneaks away before the farmers see him. They think Betsy is playing tricks. One of the sheep says, "Baaaaaad shepherdess!" Zimmo does his trick again, and Betsy has her whistle taken away and is sent back to Shepherd School. She is given one more chance. This time Zimmo charges the herd but stops short when he spots Betsy's lunch pail. She offers the wolf her lunch, and he, in turn, helps rescue some lambs who have gone over the cliff. Betsy and the wolf sing together: "Tralaa tralee. Ha ha haloo."

London, Jonathan
Froggy Gets Dressed
Illustrated by Frank Remkiewicz. Viking, 1992

Froggy wakes up in the middle of winter and decides to play outside in the snow instead of hibernating. He puts on his socks with a "zoop," his boots with a "zup," his hat with a "zat," his scarf with a "zwit," and his mittens with a "zum." "And he flopped outside into the snow—flop flop flop." His mother shouts, "Frrrrooggyy." Froggy responds, "Wha-a-a-t?" Froggy has forgotten his pants. He goes back inside and takes off each piece of clothing with the corresponding sound effect. He puts his pants on with a "zip" and marches back outside. The scenario is repeated when he forgets his shirt, coat, and underwear.

There are more than twenty books featuring Froggy. The second in the series is *Let's Go, Froggy!* (Viking, 1994).

Lowell, Susan
Dusty Locks and the Three Bears
Illustrated by Randy Cecil. Holt, 2001

The three grizzly bears go for a walk to let their red-hot beans cool. In the meantime, a dirty little girl who "hadn't had a bath for a month of Sundays" (hence her name, Dusty Locks) sneaks into the bears' cabin. She eats the cub's beans, busts his three-legged stool, and falls asleep on his bed. The bears come home. When the bear cub finds his broken chair, he exclaims, "And someone's been sitting in my chair, and smashed it all to flinders!" When the big grizzly is upset at Dusty Locks's damage, he yells, "BEAN RUSTLER! CHAIR BUSTER!" They find the intruder, who escapes out a window.

"Oops!" cried Froggy,
looking more red in the face
than green.

Froggy Gets Dressed by Jonathan London

Lum, Kate
What! Cried Granny: An Almost Bedtime Story
Illustrated by Adrian Johnson. Dial, 1999

Patrick spends the night at Granny's house, but there isn't a spare bed. "What?" cries Granny, who promptly chops down a tree, draws up some plans, and builds and paints a new bed for Patrick. The scenario repeats itself when Granny learns that Patrick also needs a pillow, blanket, and teddy bear. Your child will giggle with every incredulous "What?!?"

Massie, Diane Redfield
The Baby Beebee Bird
Illustrated by Steven Kellogg. HarperCollins, 2000

The animals in the zoo settle down for the night. The elephant yawns and nestles into the hay. "'I've eaten 562 peanuts today,' he said." The zoo is very quiet until a loud "Beebeebobbibobbi beebeebobbibobbi" wakes everyone up. It's the baby beebee bird, who is wide awake. The other animals get cranky. The baby beebee exclaims, "I've slept all day and now it's time for me to sing." The next morning, the zookeeper notices the animals lying down and worries that they're sick. Meanwhile, the baby beebee bird quiets down and falls asleep. The animals make a plan. They make a big racket and wake up the baby beebee bird. That night, all of the animals, including the baby beebee bird, sleep soundly. Please be warned: saying "baby beebee bird" aloud over and over can be addictive.

McDermott, Gerald
Zomo the Rabbit: A Trickster Tale from West Africa
Illustrated by the author. Harcourt, 1992

Zomo the rabbit is not big or strong. "But he is very clever." He asks the Sky God for wisdom. The Sky God tells Zomo he must earn wisdom. Zomo sets off to "do three impossible things." The first task is to bring back the scales of Big Fish. Zomo plays his drums and attracts Big Fish out of the sea. The fish dances so fast, his scales fall off. "Big Fish was naked." Zomo gathers the scales and embarks on task number two: to bring back the milk of Wild Cow. Zomo insults the cow and tricks it into charging at a tree. Wild Cow's horns get stuck. Zomo "turned his drum upside down and filled it with milk." For the final task, Zomo must bring back the tooth of Leopard. He succeeds and delivers all of the items to the Sky God. Zomo learns that next time he sees Big Fish, Wild Cow, or Leopard, he will have the wisdom to . . . run fast!

Companion books: *Raven: A Trickster Tale from the Pacific Northwest* (Harcourt, 1993); *Coyote: A Trickster Tale from the American Southwest* (Harcourt, 1994); *Jabutí the Tortoise: A Trickster Tale from the Amazon* (Harcourt, 2001); *Pig-Boy: A Trickster Tale from Hawai'i* (Harcourt, 2009); *Monkey: A Trickster Tale from India* (Houghton Mifflin, 2011)

McElligott, Matthew
Even Monsters Need Haircuts
Illustrated by the author. Walker, 2010

A boy sneaks into his father's barbershop in the middle of the night accompanied by a vampire. He uses a skeleton key to get in. "I unpack my supplies. The rotting tonic, horn polish, and stink wax go on the counter. The shamp-ewww goes next to the sink." He then cuts the hair of a variety of monsters, including a Cyclops, Frankenstein's monster, Medusa (the boy wears a blindfold while working on her), and a skeleton (the boy is shown looking at the skeleton's skull with a puzzled expression). Everyone is surprised when a human customer enters—until the customer removes his head and asks, "Can you take a little off the top? We all had a good laugh over that one."

McFarland, Lyn Rossiter
Widget
Illustrated by Jim McFarland. Farrar Straus Giroux, 2001

Widget, a stray dog, has no home or friends. He finds a house with "a door just his size." Inside, he sees "six cats, six warm beds, and six bowls of hot food." Mrs. Diggs's cats, "the girls," don't like the new dog. However, he confuses them, first by meowing and then by hissing, spitting, and growling. While Widget and the girls are sizing each other up, the six cats puff up, trying to intimidate the dog. Widget puffs up back at them. Later, Widget uses the litter box. Widget starts barking when Mrs. Diggs has an accident and doesn't move. The surprised cats start barking, too, and help quickly arrives. Mrs. Diggs concludes, "It's nice to have a dog. Right, girls?"

Companion book: *Widget and the Puppy* (Farrar Straus Giroux, 2004)

McMullan, Kate
I Stink!

Illustrated by Jim McMullan. HarperCollins, 2002

An anthropomorphic garbage truck with an attitude talks directly to the reader. "Know what I do at night while you're asleep? Eat your trash, that's what." He's proud of his ten wide tires, steering wheels, gas pedals, and brakes. "I am totally Dual Op." The truck is unapologetic about waking you up while collecting and compacting the garbage. The trash causes him to burp. The middle section of the picture book is an alphabetical litany of trash items, such as "Apple cores, Banana peels, Candy wrappers," all the way to "Zipped-up ziti with zucchini." He agrees that he does indeed stink. "WHOOOOO-WHEE! Do I ever! No skunk ever stunk THIS BAD!"

Companion books: *I'm Mighty!* (HarperCollins, 2003); *I'm Dirty!* (HarperCollins, 2006); *I'm Big!* (Balzer and Bray, 2010); *I'm Fast!* (Balzer and Bray, 2012)

Meddaugh, Susan
Cinderella's Rat

Illustrated by the author. Houghton Mifflin, 1997

A rat and his sister are caught in a trap. He is transformed into a coachman. "Well, more of a coachboy." He misses his tail but obediently drives Cinderella in her pumpkin coach to the ball. While Cinderella dances, the coachboy finds the castle's kitchen. "Rat heaven!" Another boy joins him but jumps up when he sees a rat. The rat turns out to be the coachboy's sister. The second boy helps them locate a wizard to turn the sister into a human girl. Instead, he turns her into a cat. When the wizard succeeds in turning her into a human, the girl starts barking. At the stroke of midnight, the coachboy turns back into a rat, but his sister remains a human. "Life is full of surprises, so you might as well get used to it."

Meddaugh, Susan
Martha Speaks

Illustrated by the author. Houghton Mifflin, 1992

Martha the dog eats a bowl of alphabet soup. Instead of going to her stomach, the letters go to her brain and give her the ability to talk to her human family.

They ask her questions like "Do dogs dream?" and "Why do you drink out of the toilet?" Martha says things like "What's all this nonsense about Pit Bulls?" and "Lassie is not all that smart." There are drawbacks to having a talking dog. "Mom says that fruitcake you sent wasn't fit for a dog. But I thought it was delicious." Martha talks so much that her family finally tells her, "Shut up!" Martha is crushed. Not until she saves the day by catching a thief does everything return to "normal."

Companion books: *Martha Calling* (Houghton Mifflin, 1994); *Martha Blah Blah* (Houghton Mifflin, 1996); *Martha Walks the Dog* (Houghton Mifflin, 1998); *Martha and Skits* (Houghton Mifflin, 2000); *Perfectly Martha* (Houghton Mifflin, 2004). There are also several adaptations based on the television series.

Miller, Sara Swan
Three Stories You Can Read to Your Dog
Illustrated by True Kelley. Houghton Mifflin, 1995

Tell your dog about the time he heard a thumping sound and he immediately thought "Burglar!" He ran to the door and went "BARK BARK ARK ARK ARK ARK ARK ARK ARK ARK ARK ARK ARK ARK ARK ARK ARK ARK ARK ARK ARK!" You opened the door to show him nobody was there. He was proud that he scared the burglar away. "Hey, good dog. Do you want another story? Here is another one just for you." The second story is about the time he buried a bone in the backyard and dreamed a bone tree had grown. In the final story, the dog wants to be a Wild Dog and scare cars and squirrels. Being a Wild Dog isn't all that great. There are no cans of dog food in the wild. "I think I will be a House Dog again."

Companion books: *Three Stories You Can Read to Your Cat* (Houghton Mifflin, 1997); *Three More Stories You Can Read to Your Dog* (Houghton Mifflin, 2000); *Three More Stories You Can Read to Your Cat* (Houghton Mifflin, 2002); *Three Stories You Can Read to Your Teddy Bear* (Houghton Mifflin, 2003)

Monks, Lydia
Aaaarrgghh! Spider!
Illustrated by the author. Houghton Mifflin, 2004

A spider wants to become a human family's pet. Unfortunately, whenever anyone spots her, they shout out "Aaaarrgghh! Spider!" The family freaks out when she shows them how good a dancer she is. Dad traps the spider and lets her go outside. She returns. She wants to prove to the humans that she's clean, so she appears in the bathtub. Mom flushes her down the drain. The spider wins them over by making several beautiful sparkly webs outside. The family takes the spider to the playground and the grocery store. There's a particularly silly picture of the spider on a leash going for a walk with the family. It's fun reading the title phrase aloud.

Monroe, Chris
Sneaky Sheep
Illustrated by the author. Carolrhoda, 2010
Blossom and Rocky try to sneak out of their meadow to reach a yummy green patch way up high on a mountainside. Their watchdog, Murphy, is very good about keeping them where they belong. In addition to the zig-zag trails the two sheep take to lose Murphy (though he always finds them), there is a double-page spread that illustrates the point, "they had been known to make some bad decisions over the years." We see Blossom and Rocky skateboarding without helmets, playing poker with those famous poker dogs, running with scissors, and running with the bulls. The two sheep see their chance to run away when Murphy is helping another sheep get her foot out of a gopher hole. Blossom and Rocky run into the woods. A wolf appears and tells the two sheep, "Don't hurry off! You just got here!" Murphy saves the day and the two sheep learn their lesson—for a while.

Most, Bernard
The Cow That Went Oink
Illustrated by the author. Harcourt, 1990
"There was once a cow that went OINK. The cows that went MOO laughed at the cow that went OINK." We see a field filled with cows all laughing, "Moo-ha." The other farm animals find this amusing and laugh in their own styles: "Neigh-ha," "Oink-ha," "Hee-haw-ha," "Cock-a-doodle-ha," and so on. The sad cow hears a friendly "MOO" coming from a pig. This pig has been the object of laughter from "the pigs that went OINK." Cow and Pig wisely ignore the other animals and keep practicing their own noises: "Oimook," "Oinkoo," "Moink," and "Mook." In the end, they wind up bilingual, each able to say both "Moo" and "Oink."

Munsch, Robert
Moira's Birthday
Illustrated by Michael Martchenko. Annick, 1987
Moira wants to invite "grade 1, grade 2, grade 3, grade 4, grade 5, grade 6, aaaaand kindergarten" to attend her birthday party. Her mother tells her that she can invite six kids. "And NNNNNO kindergarten!" After she invites six fellow students, other students beg to be invited to her party. Moira says, "Ummmmmm . . . O.K." Sure enough, on the day of her party, six kids enter Moira's house. A few moments later, there is a bigger knock and in come "grade 1, grade 2, grade 3, grade 4, grade 5, grade 6, aaaaand kindergarten." Moira's parents order two hundred pizzas and two hundred birthday cakes. They wonder who will clean up the mess. Moira decides to give one of her presents to anyone who helps clean up.

Munsch, Robert
Stephanie's Ponytail
Illustrated by Michael Martchenko. Annick, 1996

Stephanie goes to school wearing her ponytail in a different style each day. The other children (and a teacher or two) first mock her. They say "ugly, ugly, *very* ugly." But then they all show up the next day wearing the same hairstyle as Stephanie. She yells at them: "You are all a bunch of copycats." The second day, Stephanie wears a ponytail "coming out the side just above my ear." The exchange with the others repeats itself. On the third and fourth days, Stephanie wears her ponytail "coming out of the top of my head like a tree" and in front of her nose. In the end, Stephanie loudly pronounces that she is going to show up at school the next day completely bald. Everyone shows up the next day with shaven heads, except Stephanie, who is sporting a nice simple ponytail.

Munsch, Robert
Thomas' Snowsuit
Illustrated by Michael Martchenko. Annick, 1985

Thomas refuses to wear his new brown snowsuit. "If you think I am going to wear that ugly snowsuit, you are crazy!" His mother picks him up, struggles, and gets the snowsuit on Thomas. At school, his teacher tells him to put it on. Thomas replies with a loud "NNNNNO!" After a brief struggle, the teacher winds up wearing the snowsuit. Her dress ends up on Thomas. He removes the dress and is standing in his underwear when the principal walks in. There is another struggle. "When he was done, the principal was wearing the teacher's dress, the teacher was wearing the principal's suit, and Thomas was still in his underwear."

Noll, Amanda
I Need My Monster
Illustrated by Howard McWilliam. Flashlight Press, 2009

One night, a boy finds a note from the monster under his bed. It reads, "Gone fishing. Back in a week. Gabe." The boy auditions other monsters. The first monster doesn't have claws. "But I have an overbite. And I'm a mouth breather." The second monster has claws, but there's nail polish on them. "I believe professional monsters should always be well-groomed." The third monster turns out to be a girl monster wearing a pink bow on her tail. "Boy monsters are for boys and girl monsters are for girls." The next monster has a long, silly-looking tongue that makes the boy laugh. Gabe finally returns, with all the right scary features. "I shivered again. I'd be asleep in no time."

Numeroff, Laura Joffe
If You Give a Mouse a Cookie
Illustrated by Felicia Bond. HarperCollins, 1985

This may be my favorite picture book. I read it aloud so many times to so many kids that I eventually had it memorized. A young boy gives a cookie to a mouse dressed in overalls and a backpack. Consequences of this action follow. The mouse follows the boy into the house and gets a glass of milk. The mouse wants a straw. When the milk is done, he asks for a napkin and a mirror "to make sure he doesn't have a milk mustache." He notices his hair needs a trim and asks for scissors. When he gets a broom to sweep up the hair, he gets carried away and sweeps "every room in the house." He washes the floor, too, and then needs a nap. After all his exertions, the mouse becomes thirsty again. He asks for a glass of milk. "And chances are if he asks for a glass of milk, he's going to want a cookie to go with it."

Companion books: *If You Give a Moose a Muffin* (HarperCollins, 1991); *If You Give a Pig a Pancake* (HarperCollins, 1998); *If You Take a Mouse to the Movies* (HarperCollins, 2000); *If You Take a Mouse to School* (HarperCollins, 2002); *If You Give a Pig a Party* (HarperCollins, 2005); *If You Give a Cat a Cupcake* (HarperCollins, 2008); *If You Give a Dog a Donut* (Balzer and Bray, 2011)

Offill, Jenny
17 Things I'm Not Allowed to Do Anymore
Illustrated by Nancy Carpenter. Schwartz & Wade, 2007

"I had an idea to staple my brother's hair to his pillow. I'm not allowed to use the stapler anymore." This is just the first of a young girl's many naughty activities. She also glues her brother's bunny slippers to the floor and walks backward to school. She decides to do a school report on beavers instead of the required report on George Washington. She shows beavers crossing the Delaware River and tapes a picture of a beaver on a one-dollar bill. She freezes a dead fly in an ice cube, flings cauliflower at her brother, pretends her mother is a waitress and complains about the food, and shows "Joey Whipple my underpants" by doing a cartwheel.

O'Malley, Kevin
Animal Crackers Fly the Coop
Illustrated by the author. Walker, 2010

This retelling of the traditional story "The Brementown Musicians" features a wise-cracking hen. "How do comedians like their eggs? Funny-side up!" She aspires to be a "comedi-hen." When the farmer tells her she'll make a fine chicken dinner this "Fry-day," she flies the coop. Hen meets fellow comedians Dog, Cat, and Cow, and they decide to open a comedy club. They scare away some robbers and take over their house. "Now the four comedians have a comedy club. It's called COW-DOGKIT-HEN." Animals come from all over to see the shows. In addition to the animals' riddles ("Why didn't the skeleton cross the road? He didn't have the guts."), the narration is full of puns ("It didn't take much *purr*-suasion to get the cat to go with them.").

O'Malley, Kevin
Straight to the Pole
Illustrated by the author. Walker, 2003

A young child trudges through a snowstorm. As the storm gets worse, the child thinks he can't go on. "Bone-chilling winds biting my cheeks. I can't go on . . . must go on. The storm is getting worse. The ice and snow have filled up my boots." He stumbles and says, "Remember me." He panics when he sees a wolf. "I'm doomed." He musters his last ounce of strength and hollers, "WON'T SOMEONE SAVE ME?" We then see that he has crawled to a bus stop sign, where he is joined by his friends. The wolf is a dog. The atmosphere changes to joy when he learns that school has been canceled. Adults will particularly enjoy seeing the images of the boy bravely facing the elements as he wades knee-deep in snow.

Palatini, Margie
Bad Boys
Illustrated by Henry Cole. Katherine Tegen, 2003

Willy and Wally Wolf—the "bad boys" as in "big bad wolves"—are running away from Little Red Riding Hood and the Three Little Pigs. They hide themselves in a flock of sheep—"two wolves in sheep's clothing" with the intention of eating the sheep. The wolves brag that they'll "Pull the wool over their eyes." They put on woolly long johns, mascara, and stockings and introduce themselves as "Willimina and Wallanda . . . the Peep Sheep." They meet a sheep named Meryl Sheep. Old Betty Mutton isn't fooled, however. "I knew the Peep Sheep. I grazed with the Peep Sheep. And you two don't leap like the Peep Sheep." Betty tricks the bad boys into getting sheared by the farmers.

    Companion books: *Bad Boys Get Cookie!* (Katherine Tegen, 2006); *Bad Boys Get Henpecked!* (Katherine Tegen, 2009)

Palatini, Margie
Piggie Pie!
Illustrated by Howard Fine. Clarion, 1995

Gritch the Witch's piggie pie recipe calls for eight plump piggies. She heads over the river and through the woods to Old MacDonald's farm (she sees an ad in the yellow pages instructing her to call EI-EI-O). The pigs disguise themselves as ducks, cows, chickens, and Old MacDonald himself. Since the pigs are undercover as other animals, they "quack-quack here" and "moo-moo there" and "cluck-cluck everywhere." Gritch runs into a wolf, who complains, "I've been chasing three little pigs for days." Gritch invites the wolf for dinner, imagining him between two pieces of bread. The wolf, meanwhile, is imagining the witch in a hamburger bun. There is a great illustration where the witch is flying overhead on her broom, spelling out "Surrender Piggies," in a reference to the movie *The Wizard of Oz*.

Companion books: *Zoom Broom* (Hyperion, 1998); *Broom Mates* (Hyperion, 2003)

Peet, Bill
Chester, the Worldly Pig
Illustrated by the author. Houghton Mifflin, 1965

Chester learns to do a trick with his flat pig snout. He can balance himself on his nose. He runs away and joins a circus but is dismayed when the circus people put him in the tiger cage for "an element of danger." Chester faints and later is given a job with a clown. That's not what he signed up for, so once again Chester runs away. A bear chases Chester, who runs into a trio of tramps who want to eat him for dinner. Chester escapes into the city, but "it was plain to see that the big city was no place for a pig." He walks back out to the countryside, where a farmer fattens him up for slaughter. On the day "this little piggy goes to market," a traveling showman buys Chester because he notices something unique about the pig. There, on his side, is a pattern on his skin of "the entire map of the world."

Pilkey, Dav
'Twas the Night before Thanksgiving
Illustrated by the author. Orchard, 1990

Eight children and their teacher take a school field trip to a farm. They meet Farmer Mack Nuggett and his eight turkeys: "Now Ollie, now Stanley, now Larry and Moe, / On Wally, on Beaver, on Shemp and Groucho!" The children are shocked to learn that Farmer Nuggett plans to use his ax on the turkeys. The children start crying. Farmer Nuggett and the teacher rush to the well to fetch the children some water. When they return, the two adults fail to notice that the children are "mysteriously fatter" (we can see turkey feathers poking out from under the children's jackets). "The very next evening, / Eight families were blessed / With eight fluffy / Thanksgiving turkeys / As guests."

Pinkwater, Daniel
Bad Bears in the Big City
Illustrated by Jill Pinkwater. Houghton Mifflin, 2003

Two polar bears—Irving and Muktuk—arrive at the zoo in chains. "They are not to be trusted." They are shown to their rooms and they meet their roommate Roy, "the other polar bear." Roy has an apartment he goes to each night. The three of them eat bear chow but long for muffins from the nearby muffin factory. One night, after Roy checks out (we see him at a time clock), Irving and Muktuk plan their escape. They eventually disguise themselves and join a tour of the muffin factory. They get in trouble for leaving the zoo, but

Roy promises to watch them. "They are bad bears, I have to say it . . . But they have assured me they will not eat people."

Companion books: *Irving and Muktuk: Two Bad Bears* (Houghton Mifflin, 2001); *Bad Bears and a Bunny* (Houghton Mifflin, 2005); *Bad Bear Detectives* (Houghton Mifflin, 2006); *Bad Bears Go Visiting* (Houghton Mifflin, 2007)

Plourde, Lynn
Pajama Day
Illustrated by Thor Wickstrom. Dutton, 2005

Everyone in Mrs. Shepherd's class shows up clad appropriately for Pajama Day except for a student named Drew A. Blank. "Drew had forgotten what day it was. In fact, Drew might have forgotten his own name if it hadn't been written on his hand as a reminder." Drew has also forgotten his slippers, breakfast snack, teddy bear, and pillow but comes up with creative substitutes. He rummages in the lost-and-found pile and finds two "slippers" so he can join the morning meeting circle (the slippers are a glove and a mitten). He has several after-school activities. He's so exhausted at the end of the day that he forgets to put on his pajamas for bed.

Companion books: *School Picture Day* (Dutton, 2002); *Teacher Appreciation Day* (Dutton, 2003); *Book Fair Day* (Dutton, 2006); *Science Fair Day* (Dutton, 2008); *Field Trip Day* (Dutton, 2010)

Proimos, James
Swim! Swim!
Illustrated by the author. Scholastic, 2010

Lerch, a pet fish, tells his story of looking for a friend. First, he spots some pebbles at the bottom of his tank and asks, "Pebbles, will you be my friend?" After getting no response, he spots a fishbowl deep-sea diver and asks, "Sir, would you be my friend?" Thinking the diver is rejecting him, Lerch starts crying. "Good thing you can't see tears underwater." Next, Lerch hears bubbles and tries to talk to them. "I'll try talking bubble." A cat shows up outside Lerch's tank. The cat mistakes Lerch's name for "lunch." The cat moves Lerch to another tank, where Lerch meets Dinah (or as the cat says, "dinner"). The two fish enjoy each other's company immensely.

Pulver, Robin
Author Day for Room 3T
Illustrated by Chuck Richards. Clarion, 2005

Harry Bookman, the author of *The Banana from Outer Space, Ants in My Lunch Box*, and *The Mystery of the Missing Monkey Bars*, is coming to visit the students in Room 3T. They are excited but aren't exactly sure what he looks like (the images they conjure range from space traveler to superhero). A chimpanzee enters the class and the children assume he is Harry Bookman. Their teacher has inconveniently lost her glasses and doesn't suspect anything's wrong.

"The author jumped up and down. He scooped ice cubes out of his water and tossed them everywhere. He panted and hooted in a raspy voice. 'Oh, dear,' said the librarian. 'Apparently, Harry Bookman has laryngitis.'" One teacher tells the class, "no monkey business." We see many of the children looking and behaving like monkeys. After a lady from a television show retrieves the chimpanzee, the real author shows up and says, "Harry Bookman." "'Sorry,' said Skippy. 'He just left.'"

Pulver, Robin
Axle Annie
Illustrated by Tedd Arnold. Dial, 1999

Axle Annie is a modern tall-tale character who drives a school bus. She never fails to deliver the kids to school, even on the snowiest days. She always makes it up Tiger Hill, and "that's why the schools in Burskyville never had a snow day." This makes Shifty Rhodes, another bus driver, angry. He wants a snow day. One day, the radio announces the school closings around the area and adds that only one school remains open. "'Don't say Burskyville!' pleaded Shifty. 'Burksyville,' said the radio." Shifty plots to add even more snow to Tiger Hill with a snowmaking machine. Axle Annie finds that she needs help with this challenge.

Companion book: *Axle Annie and the Speed Grump* (Dial, 2005)

Ransom, Jeanie Franz
What Really Happened to Humpty?
Illustrated by Stephen Axelsen. Charlesbridge, 2009

When Humpty Dumpty falls off the wall, his brother Joe investigates. When Joe finds Humpty on the ground, Muffy (Little Miss Muffet) says, "At least he landed sunny-side up." Joe is so mad, he says that whoever did this is "gonna fry." Mother Goose tells Joe that Humpty's fall was an accident. "There's no case to crack." Joe works his way around Mother Gooseland, interviewing everyone from Goldilocks to Old Mother Hubbard. He learns a big wind occurred at the same time that both the Three Pigs' new house went down and Humpty took his spill. Joe Dumpty solves the case, which involves both the Big Bad Wolf and Muffy.

Rathmann, Peggy
Good Night, Gorilla
Illustrated by the author. Putnam, 1994

It's the end of the day and the zookeeper says, "Good night, Gorilla." The small gorilla snitches the zookeeper's key and follows the zookeeper as he says good night to the other animals. The gorilla unlocks the cages of the elephant, lion, hyena, giraffe, and armadillo. Instead of fleeing, the animals follow the unsuspecting zookeeper back to his house. They settle down for the night in the zookeeper's bedroom. The gorilla climbs into bed next to the zookeeper's wife. The animals aren't discovered until they all reply to the wife's "Good night." The zookeeper's wife leads all of the animals back to their cages. The gorilla manages to sneak out again. Sharp-eyed kids will notice a little mouse and its banana in every illustration. The book contains very few words, but many laughs.

Rathmann, Peggy
Officer Buckle and Gloria
Illustrated by the author. Putnam, 1995

Officer Buckle is not the most successful safety officer. We first meet him getting an idea for a new safety tip—"NEVER stand on a SWIVEL CHAIR"— while he is falling from standing on a swivel chair. Police dog Gloria helps perk up Officer Buckle's boring safety-school programs by acting out each safety tip behind his back. Her actions are very funny. Officer Buckle tells the children, "NEVER leave a THUMBTACK where you might SIT on it." Gloria is seen jumping up in the air holding her rear end. The two have a falling out but get back together when Officer Buckle remembers "Safety Tip #101: ALWAYS STICK WITH YOUR BUDDY!" Be sure to point out the various safety tips on the front and back endpapers, such as "Never put anything in your nose" (accompanied by a picture of Gloria with a banana in her nose).

Rex, Adam
Pssst!
Illustrated by the author. Harcourt, 2007

A girl is walking through the zoo when she hears the title sound, "Pssst!" A gorilla wants her to find him a new tire. His old tire swing is broken. The girl says, "Well . . . I guess so." She moves on. She hears the noise again. A boar wants her to bring a trash can. The girl hears requests from bats, a hippo, penguins, sloths, turkeys, a baboon, a tortoise, and a peacock. "Luckily there was a store across the street that sold everything." The animals use the items to make their escape from the zoo. The background illustrations are full of wonderful images and signs. We see a small deer in a deer-sized hamster ball in one picture, and a few pages later we see a rhino in another (much larger) hamster ball. A walrus is sitting behind a sign that reads, "I am the walrus (koo-koo-kachoo)."

Roberton, Fiona
Wanted: The Perfect Pet
Illustrated by the author. Putnam, 2010

Henry wants a dog so badly that he pays for an advertisement in the classifieds of *The Daily Catastrophe*. A lonely duck spots the ad, dresses up as a dog, and shows up at the boy's front door. "'A dog!' yelled Henry. 'Woof!' said the duck." They play, although the duck has trouble catching balls and learning new tricks. When the dog costume falls off, Henry is stunned. Then he gives "the duck a nice hot bath and a cup of tea." He does research on ducks and learns good things about them. Ducks don't get dog breath, "won't eat homework, chew shoes or furniture, *and* won't pee on the carpet." He calls the duck Spot. "'Quack,' said Spot."

Root, Phyllis
Creak! Said the Bed
Illustrated by Regan Dunnick. Candlewick, 2010
When little Evie opens her parents' bedroom door, it goes, "Squeak." Evie is afraid and wants to sleep in her parents' bed. Her father snores and her mother says, "Sure!" This starts a procession of family members climbing into the bed. Ivy is freezing, Mo is afraid, and even Fred the dog wants to join them. Poppa, who has been delivering a variety of snoring sounds, sits up and says, "There's no more room for Fred in the bed!" Fred jumps up anyway, and the bed breaks with a "Crack." The book ends with everyone asleep and the floor making creaking noises as cracks start to appear.

Schneider, Howie
Chewy Louie
Illustrated by the author. Rising Moon, 2000
Father brings home a puppy. He's always very hungry, so they name him Chewy Louie. "He ate everything we put in his bowl. Then he ate the bowl." They get him a new bowl and he eats that one, too. He eats the little boy's toys and his "trains before they reached the station. Then he ate the station." When Louie starts eating the back porch, they take him to the vet. They vet tells them that he's just growing. As they drive away, we see bites out of the car, the furniture in the vet's office, and the vet's pants. The family hires a dog trainer. Louie eats the trainer's cane. They hire a musician to sing "songs to Louie about the error of his ways." Louie eats the musician's guitar. Finally, the family notices that Louie has stopped chewing everything in sight. "He's not a puppy anymore." We then see that the back endpaper has a "bite" taken out of it.

Scieszka, Jon
The Frog Prince, Continued
Illustrated by Steve Johnson. Viking, 1991
The book begins with a recap of "The Princess and the Frog": the princess kissed the frog, who turned into a prince, and they lived happily ever after. "Okay, so they weren't so happy. In fact, they were miserable." The princess complains about the prince's nasty habit of sticking out his tongue. He complains that she never wants to go down to the pond. When she tells him that she thinks they would be better off if he were still a frog, he runs "into the forest, looking for a witch who could turn him back into a frog." The first witch thinks about casting a spell on him so he can't wake up Sleeping Beauty. The second witch offers him what's obviously a poisoned apple. The third witch invites him into her house, with its gingerbread windowsill. "Do you happen

to know any children by the name of Hansel and Gretel?" he asks. "Why yes, Prince darling, I do. I'm expecting them for dinner." The prince knows his fairy tales and once again runs away. He finally arrives home and kisses the princess. "They both turned into frogs. And they hopped off happily ever after."

Scieszka, Jon
Squids Will Be Squids: Fresh Morals, Beastly Fables
Illustrated by Lane Smith. Viking, 1998

According to the author, "This is a collection of fables that Aesop might have told if he were alive today and sitting in the back of class daydreaming and goofing around." The opening fable is titled "Grasshopper Logic." Grasshopper waits until the last minute to do his homework. His mother is upset about the amount of homework. When she asks Grasshopper how long he has known about these assignments, he tells her that he doesn't know. The moral of the story is "There are plenty of things to say to calm a hopping mad Grasshopper Mom. 'I don't know' is not one of them." Other fables follow the exploits of a frog with new skateboard shoes, a flatulent skunk, a truthful walrus child, a Piece of Toast and Froot Loops "arguing over who was loved the most," and more.

Scieszka, Jon
The Stinky Cheese Man and Other Fairly Stupid Tales
Illustrated by Lane Smith. Viking, 1992

Jack of "Jack and the Beanstalk" fame narrates several fractured versions of popular fairy tales. He is pestered by the Little Red Hen, who complains about the author and illustrator. Chicken Licken worries that the sky is falling. It turns out that the table of contents is falling and, indeed, it squashes the characters from that story. Another story combines the characters from "Cinderella" and "Rumpelstiltskin" and is titled "Cinderumpelstiltskin." The ugly duckling grows up to be "just a really ugly duck." Little Red Riding Hood and the Big Bad Wolf leave their story because they don't like how Jack is telling it. The title story is a retelling of "The Gingerbread Man," but in this case, no one wants to chase the Stinky Cheese Man. "'I'm not really very hungry,' said the little old man. 'I'm not really all that lonely,' said the little old lady."

Scieszka, Jon
The True Story of the Three Little Pigs
Illustrated by Lane Smith. Viking, 1989

The wolf from "The Three Little Pigs" tells his side of the story. "I don't know how this whole Big Bad Wolf thing got started, but it's all wrong." He ran out of sugar as he was baking a cake for his "dear old granny." He walked over to borrow a cup of sugar from his neighbor in the straw house. Instead of huffing and puffing to blow the house down, the wolf huffed and puffed because he had a cold. He blew the house over by accident. The pig died, so the wolf ate it. He thought it would be wasteful to leave the pig. "Think of it as a big cheeseburger just lying there." The same thing happened with the second pig. When the third pig insulted the wolf's granny, the wolf huffed and puffed in anger until the police arrived. "The rest, as they say, is history."

Seuss, Dr.
Horton Hatches the Egg
Illustrated by the author. Random House, 1940
Mayzie, a lazy bird, asks Horton the elephant to sit on her egg. He sits on the egg in all sorts of weather, through the fall and the winter. Horton does not abandon the egg because "an elephant's faithful—one hundred percent." A group of hunters finds Horton, and they are amazed at the sight of an elephant in a tree. They capture Horton and sell him to the circus, tree and all. Mayzie happens upon the circus and spots Horton. At that moment, the egg starts to hatch. Mayzie claims the egg, but when it bursts open, a tiny flying elephant appears. The circus audience cheers at the sight of the new Elephant-Bird.
    Companion book: *Horton Hears a Who!* (Random House, 1954)

Seuss, Dr.
The Sneetches and Other Stories
Illustrated by the author. Random House, 1961
We meet the Star-Belly Sneetches, who think they are better than the Plain-Belly Sneetches. "You could only play if your bellies had stars / And the Plain-Belly children had none upon thars." They are all swindled by Sylvester McMonkey McBean, who bills himself as a "Fix-It-Up Chappie." In the end, the Sneetches agree that "Sneetches are Sneetches / And no kind of Sneetch is the best on the beaches." The book also includes a story about the North-Going Zak who confronts the equally stubborn South-Going Zak, a spooky story featuring "the pants with nobody inside 'em," and a story about a woman who has twenty-three sons named Dave. Have fun reading all of the wild names she should have considered, such as Putt-Putt, Stinkey, Moon Face, Marvin O'Gravel Balloon Face, Oliver Bolivar Butt, and Zanzibar Buck-Buck McFate.

Seuss, Dr.
Yertle the Turtle and Other Stories
Illustrated by the author. Random House, 1958
Yertle the Turtle is the king of a pond. Everyone seems happy except for Yertle. He wants to rule higher up. He forces turtles to stack themselves on top of one another to make a new throne. Mack, the turtle on the bottom, complains about his pains. Yertle shouts "Silence!" and orders more turtles to make a higher throne. After getting upset that the moon is higher than he is, Yertle orders about "five thousand, six hundred and seven" more turtles. Before they arrive, Mack burps and Yertle plummets. "And today, the great Yertle, that Marvelous he, / Is King of the Mud. That is all he can see." Another story

features a rabbit who claims he can hear a fly cough ninety miles away, a bear who claims he can smell a stale egg more than six hundred miles away, and a worm who claims to be able to see all the way around the entire world until he sees "the two biggest fools that have ever been seen!"

Shannon, David
Duck on a Bike
Illustrated by the author. Blue Sky, 2002
Duck finds a boy's red bike and begins to ride it around the farm. The other farm animals react in different ways. The cow thinks, "A duck on a bike? That's the silliest thing I've ever seen!" The sheep is worried about the duck's safety. The cat couldn't care less, while the dog thinks, "it's a mighty neat trick." The chicken is startled and the goat wants to eat the bike. The pigs think Duck is a show-off. A group of kids ride their bikes to the farm and disappear inside the farmhouse. All of the farm animals have wide-eyed, bright looks on their faces. Soon, they are all riding the bikes. The picture of the chicken riding a tricycle is worth the price of the book. At the end of the book, Duck is eyeing a tractor.

Shannon, David
No, David!
Illustrated by the author. Blue Sky, 1998
Hilarious, double-page spreads show young David (who is based on the author's childhood memories) getting into trouble. The book opens with a picture of David's mother (shown from the waist down) tapping her foot. On the next page David is coloring on the walls. Other images show David tracking mud into the house, running down the street in his birthday suit, banging on a frying pan, jumping on his bed while wearing cowboy boots, sticking his finger up his nose (Shannon thoughtfully provides a close-up of this picture), playing baseball in the living room, and chewing with his mouth wide open. After constantly yelling "No, David!" to her son, David's mom assures him in the end that she does love him.

Companion books: *David Goes to School* (Blue Sky, 1999); *David Gets in Trouble* (Blue Sky, 2002); *It's Christmas, David!* (Blue Sky, 2010). There are also a handful of board books featuring a toddler version of David.

Shaw, Nancy
Sheep in a Jeep
Illustrated by Margot Apple. Houghton Mifflin, 1986
"Beep! Beep! Sheep in a jeep on a hill that's steep." The red jeep stalls and the five sheep hop out. "Sheep shove. Sheep grunt." The jeep heads down the hill and right into a mud puddle. The sheep try to pull the jeep out with a rope. "Sheep yelp. Sheep get help." Some pigs come to the rescue and push the jeep up on dry land. The sheep hop back in the jeep and cheer so much that the driver forgets to steer. They crash the jeep into a tree. It falls to pieces. "Jeep for

sale—cheap." You can see how simple words and short sentences can still hold humor for the very young and their parents.

Companion books: *Sheep on a Ship* (Houghton Mifflin, 1989); *Sheep in a Shop* (Houghton Mifflin, 1991); *Sheep Out to Eat* (Houghton Mifflin, 1992); *Sheep Take a Hike* (Houghton Mifflin, 1994); *Sheep Trick or Treat* (Houghton Mifflin, 1997); *Sheep Blast Off!* (Houghton Mifflin, 2008)

Shea, Bob
I'm a Shark
Illustrated by the author. Balzer and Bray, 2011

A shark brags about how awesome he is. He watches scary movies without closing his eyes (the movie on the screen shows a young human boy fishing). He doesn't cry when he gets a shot from the doctor (the needle is a swordfish). And if a dinosaur saw him, it would be scared. There's one thing the shark is afraid of—spiders. When a crab asks the shark if he's afraid of big mean bears, the shark asks, "Is the big mean bear holding a creepy spider?" When assured that the big mean bear does not have a spider, the shark says, "A big, mean, spiderless bear? Don't make me laugh!"

Sherry, Kevin
I'm the Biggest Thing in the Ocean
Illustrated by the author. Dial, 2007

A giant blue squid brags about his size, while taking up much of each double-page spread in this oversized picture book. We see the squid in comparison to shrimp, clams, a crab, a jellyfish, turtles, an octopus, a shark, and "this fish, that fish, this fish, and that fish." The giant squid doesn't look so big once a whale appears. The whale swallows the stunned squid, who finds himself in the whale's stomach with other sea creatures. He quickly regains his composure, however, and proudly declares, "I'm the biggest thing in this whale!" Be sure to share the fun dialogue on the front flap of the book jacket. The giant squid says, "Maybe you haven't noticed but I'm pretty BIG. I'm bigger than this page! I'm bigger than this book!"

Companion book: *I'm the Best Artist in the Ocean* (Dial, 2008)

Sierra, Judy
Tell the Truth, B. B. Wolf
Illustrated by J. Otto Seibold. Knopf, 2010

B. B. Wolf (of "The Three Little Pigs") attempts to tell his side of the story, but he is shouted down by the pigs in the fairy-tale audience. The wolf tells everyone that the second pig was playing with matches. That's why the wolf huffed and puffed, "To put out the flames, you understand." Pinocchio thinks the wolf's snout is getting longer. The wolf eventually apologizes, calls himself "Big Bodacious Benevolent Bookish Wolf," and helps build the pigs their "very own piggyback mansion." There are some fun Tom Swifties in the text: "'No one is falling for your story," cracked Humpty Dumpty." At one point, the wolf's cell phone goes off with a "Who's Afraid of the Big Bad Wolf?" ringtone.

Companion book: *Mind Your Manners, B. B. Wolf* (Knopf, 2007)

Silverstein, Shel
Who Wants a Cheap Rhinoceros?
Illustrated by the author. Macmillan, 1964

Someone is selling a rhinoceros and pitching the advantages of owning one. He can be used for a coat hanger—we see a person tossing his hat and coat at the rhino's horn. He's a good back scratcher with that horn of his. The same horn can "open beer cans for your uncle," stack doughnuts for grandmother, plow a field "if you are a farmer," imitate a shark, and play "records if you have no phonograph." You can also tie one end of a jump rope to the horn. The rhino's size can come in handy when you are "collecting extra allowance from your father" and discouraging your mother from punishing you. The rhino makes a good-sized "unsinkable battleship" and can even hide behind a skinny hat rack when playing hide-and-seek. Finally, "he is easy to love."

Slobodkina, Esphyr
Caps for Sale: A Tale of a Peddler, Some Monkeys, and Their Monkey Business
Illustrated by the author. Scott, 1940

A peddler displays his wares on top of his head. He goes around calling, "Caps! Caps for sale! Fifty cents a cap!" He is not selling any caps one day, so he heads out of town and takes a nap. When he wakes up, he finds that the only cap on his head is the checkered cap. Several monkeys have taken his other caps. The peddler shakes his finger at the monkeys in the trees and says, "You give me back my caps." The monkeys shake their fingers and reply, "'Tsz, tsz, tsz." The peddler shakes both hands and repeats his statement. The monkeys reply in kind. The peddler stamps his foot. The monkeys stamp their feet. The peddler grows so angry that he stamps both feet and yells, "You monkeys, you! You must give me back my caps!" The monkeys stamp both of their feet and say, "Tsz, tsz, tsz." The peddler throws his checkered cap on the ground. He's surprised and delighted to see each monkey pull off its cap and throw it to the ground. The peddler gathers the caps, puts them back in a stack on his head, and walks back to town calling, "Caps! Caps for sale! Fifty cents a cap!"

Companion book: *Circus Caps for Sale* (HarperCollins, 2002)

Small, David
George Washington's Cows
Illustrated by the author. Farrar Straus Giroux, 1994

George Washington's cows stay upstairs in a bedroom, "dressed in lavender gowns and bedded on cushions of silk." They are fed jam and cream scones and "sprayed with expensive colognes." Otherwise, they would refuse to give milk. George Washington's hogs, on the other hand, help with the household chores such as cleaning and cooking. They don jackets and wigs and "serve . . . the dinner precisely at eight." Afterward, they are seen playing music. "George Washington's sheep were all scholars." They wear graduation gowns and mortarboards and give lectures. Instead of being impressed, George Washington is sad about his animals. The book ends with him crossing the Delaware River in that famous pose, saying, "Sell the farm, I'll try politics!"

Small, David
Imogene's Antlers
Illustrated by the author. Crown, 1985

"On Thursday, Imogene woke up and found she had grown antlers." She discovers how hard it is to get through a normal day with large antlers on her head. Her clothing gets stuck on her antlers, and it's hard to fit through the door. When Imogene gets her antlers caught in the chandelier, her mother cries "OH!" and faints. The mother faints again when Imogene's brother declares that she has "turned into a rare form of miniature elk." Having antlers also turns out to be helpful. The maid dries the towels on Imogene's antlers. The cook places doughnuts on the antlers to be fed to the birds outside. "You'll be lots of fun to decorate come Christmas." Her mother continues to faint at the sight of her daughter. At the end of the book, Imogene wakes up to find her antlers gone. Instead, she is sporting a peacock's tail.

Smith, Lane
It's a Book
Illustrated by the author. Roaring Brook, 2010

A jackass asks a monkey about the item he's holding. The monkey replies, "It's a book." The jackass asks a series of questions about this book. "How do you scroll down?" "Does it need a password?" When the jackass asks, "Where's your mouse?" a tiny rodent appears from under the monkey's hat. The monkey shows the jackass a page from the book. Long John Silver is pulling out his sword and laughing at Jim. Jim sees a ship in the distance and smiles. The jackass decides there are too many letters and "fixes" the text so that it now reads, "LJS: rrr! K? lol! JIM: :(! :)" Of course, the jackass becomes engrossed with the book, and the monkey decides to go to the library. At the end of the book, the mouse gets to say a line few authors have the clout to get away with: "It's a book, Jackass."

Smith, Lane
John, Paul, George, and Ben
Illustrated by the author. Hyperion, 2006

Smith plays off the Beatles' names to teach us funny facts about the Sons of Liberty: John Hancock, Paul Revere, George Washington, Ben Franklin, and Thomas Jefferson. They are all portrayed as children who had habits we associate with their grown-up lives. John Hancock fills an entire school chalkboard with his signature. Ben Franklin comes up with so many "wise sayings that his acquaintances came up with one of their own—'Please shut your big yap!'" Paul Revere hollers while helping a woman at the store where he works: "EXTRA-LARGE UNDERWEAR? SURE WE HAVE SOME! LET'S SEE, LARGE . . . LARGE . . . EXTRA-LARGE! HERE THEY ARE! GREAT, BIG, EXTRA-LARGE UNDERWEAR!" Smith also includes a chart in the back of the book, "Wherein we set the record straight with ye olde True or False section."

Solheim, James
Born Yesterday: The Diary of a Young Journalist
Illustrated by Simon James. Philomel, 2010

A newborn baby makes several observations about his or her (we never know its gender) world. The baby is fascinated by Big Sister, who can play the harmonica, "an important life skill." Baby is impatient to grow up and go to school. After all, even the dog, Foofy, gets to go to a school. Baby has an epiphany. "Finally—I have it figured out. Some things are noses, some are taxicabs, and some are Belgians." After worrying about his/her relationship with Big Sister, Baby is startled to hear her say, "You are my best friend." Baby then admits, "I was so relieved that I tried to eat her hair."

Spinelli, Eileen
Silly Tilly
Illustrated by David Slonim. Marshall Cavendish, 2009

Tilly is a fun-loving goose, "a daffy-down-and-dilly goose who took her baths in apple juice." The goose often irritates the other farm animals with her antics. She tickles the frogs and sits on Rooster's birthday cake. When the animals first yell at Tilly, she is wearing ancient Egyptian gear and "walking like an Egyptian." They tell her that they're tired of her silly stuff. "No more naps in Scarecrow's pants! No packing Piglet off to France!" Tilly sadly stops her antics. After a while the other animals notice they haven't laughed in a long time, not since Tilly sneezed "and blew the fleas from Farmer's coat and set his underwear afloat." They complain, "It's dullsville on the farm. No fun!" They apologize to Tilly and she goes back to her old ways. We see her soaking "her feet in mayonnaise" and sledding "downhill on cookie trays."

Steig, William
Doctor De Soto
Illustrated by the author. Farrar Straus Giroux, 1982

Doctor De Soto is a good dentist. He treats many animals. But because he's a mouse, there are certain animals he refuses to treat. His sign reads, "CATS & OTHER DANGEROUS ANIMALS NOT ACCEPTED FOR TREATMENT." A well-dressed fox shows up at the office. His head is bandaged. Doctor De Soto takes pity and allows the fox in. He yanks out the fox's old rotten tooth and makes him a new one. While having his tooth repaired, the fox dreams about how good the dentist will taste. He mumbles aloud, "How I love them raw . . . with just a pinch of salt, and a . . . dry . . . white wine." Doctor De Soto glues the fox's jaws shut with a secret formula. "You won't be able to open your mouth for a day or two." The fox is helpless to do anything except mutter, "Frank oo berry mush."

Companion book: *Doctor De Soto Goes to Africa* (HarperCollins, 1992)

Steig, William
Pete's a Pizza
Illustrated by the author. HarperCollins, 1998

Pete's in a bad mood because it's raining outside and he's stuck indoors. His father "thinks it might cheer Pete up to be made into a pizza." He puts Pete down on a table and starts rolling him as if he were dough. Mother comes over and observes. Next, Father stretches "the dough" this way and that and then tosses Pete into the air. Next, oil (water) and flour (talcum powder) are applied. The toppings include tomatoes (checkers) and cheese (pieces of paper). "When the dough gets tickled, it laughs like crazy." The pizza makers tell the pizza that "pizzas are not supposed to laugh." The pizza replies that pizzas are not supposed to be tickled. Father puts the pizza in the oven (on the sofa). The pizza runs away before he's sliced. Just then, the sun comes out and "the pizza decides to go look for his friends."

Stein, David Ezra
Interrupting Chicken
Illustrated by the author. Candlewick, 2010

Papa begins reading a bedtime story to Little Red Chicken. She promises not to interrupt. However, once Papa starts reading "Hansel and Gretel," Little Red Chicken interrupts, shouting, "Don't go in! She's a witch!" Papa switches stories and begins reading "Little Red Riding Hood." Little Red Chicken once again interrupts: "Don't talk to strangers!" She does it one more time when Papa reads the story "Chicken Little." Papa is flabbergasted. The characters in the stories also react to Little Red Chicken's interruptions. Hansel and Gretel are startled, as is the witch, who is wearing an apron that reads "Kid Soup." The wolf in "Little Red Riding Hood" falls down, and the various fowl in "Chicken Little" lose a feather or two. When Little Red Chicken begins reading Papa a story titled "Bedtime for Papa," he falls asleep.

Stevens, Janet
Tops and Bottoms
Illustrated by the author. Harcourt, 1995

Here's my favorite trickster tale. Bear is lazy and lets the family farm fall to ruin. Hare and his wife cook up a plan to take advantage of the situation. Hare tells Bear that he and his family will do all the work raising crops in the field.

All Bear has to do is sleep. Hare asks if Bear wants the top half or the bottom half. Bear yawns and says the top half. Later, when the crops are harvested, Hare keeps the bottoms of the carrots, radishes, and beets, and gives Bear the tops of those vegetables. Bear tells Hare to plant the field again and give him the bottoms this time. Hare and his family do so. They keep the tops of the lettuce, broccoli, and celery and give Bear the bottoms. Bear tells them to plant the field once more and to give him both the tops and the bottoms. Hare and his family keep the middles of the next crop—the corn. Bear gets the tops (the tassels) and the bottoms (the stalks). Bear decides, "From now on, I'll plant my own crops and take the tops, bottoms, and middles!" That's okay with the Hare family. They have enough crops to open a vegetable stand.

Stevenson, James
Could Be Worse!
Illustrated by the author. Greenwillow, 1977

The kids are fairly bored at Grandpa's house. Everything is the same, day after day. Whenever one of the kids complains about something, Grandpa says, "Could be worse." One day, he overhears his grandkids talking about how nothing interesting ever happens to Grandpa. Grandpa shows up at breakfast with an elaborate tall tale. He tells them about a large bird that snatched him out of bed the previous night and dropped him in the mountains. An abominable snowman threw a huge snowball at Grandpa. He rolled into the desert, where "I got squished by a giant something-or-other." He was also kicked by an ostrich and caught by a giant lobster at the bottom of the ocean. Finally, he made a paper airplane out of a giant newspaper and flew back to bed. When he asks the kids what they think of that, they respond "Could be worse!"

There are more than ten books featuring Grandpa and his grandchildren. The second in the series is *That Terrible Halloween Night* (Greenwillow, 1980).

Stoeke, Janet Morgan
Minerva Louise
Illustrated by the author. Dutton, 1988

Minerva Louise is a chicken who loves "the house with the red curtains." She hops in through an open window and explores the house. She decides that the fireplace is a perfect nest, the flowerpot is a comfortable chair, the sleeping cat is a friendly cow, and a tricycle is a tractor. The flower pattern of a bedspread makes her think that she's looking at a meadow. She ponders why there is no one else around (we see a woman, a man, and a dog in the background). She asks a rubber duck floating in the bathtub, "Will you play with me?" She decides to rejoin her friends in the flock outside. She promises to return, and when she sees the woman putting a pie on the windowsill to cool, Minerva Louise sits on it.

Companion books: *A Hat for Minerva Louise* (Dutton, 1994); *Minerva Louise at School* (Dutton, 1996); *A Friend for Minerva Louise* (Dutton, 1997); *Minerva Louise at the Fair* (Dutton, 2000); *Minerva Louise and the*

Red Truck (Dutton, 2002); *Minerva Louise and the Colorful Eggs* (Dutton, 2006); *Minerva Louise on Christmas Eve* (Dutton, 2007); *Minerva Louise on Halloween* (Dutton, 2009)

Stone, Jon
The Monster at the End of This Book
Illustrated by Michael Smollin. Golden Books, 1971

Grover of Sesame Street talks directly to the reader, pleading, "If you do not turn any pages, we will never get to the end of this book." Grover does not want to run into the monster at the end of the book. "So please do not turn the page." On the next page, Grover slaps his forehead and cries out, "YOU TURNED THE PAGE!" Grover tries hard to prevent the reader from turning the page. He ties the pages with rope, nails the pages shut, and builds a brick wall. The pages keep getting turned, and Grover panics. "Do you know that you are very strong?" When Grover finds out that HE is the monster at the end of the book, he says, "I told you and told you there was nothing to be afraid of."

Sturges, Philemon
The Little Red Hen (Makes a Pizza)
Illustrated by Amy Walrod. Dutton, 1999

The Little Red Hen is hungry. She looks at her pantry shelf, which contains "King Kow Condensed Milk," dolphin-safe tuna, and a can of worms. She sees tomato sauce and says, "Why don't I make a lovely little pizza?" She yells out the window and asks if anyone has a pizza pan she can borrow. "'Not I,' said the duck. 'Not I,' said the dog. 'Not I,' said the cat." She heads to the store and buys a pizza pan and "some other stuff" (plant food, a yardstick, a plant, a book titled *The Do It Yourself Guide to Sink Installation*, and more). The same thing happens when she needs flour and mozzarella (she brings back "some other stuff" each time). No one will help her make the dough or the topping. At last, the pizza is done. "It was lovely, but it was not little." She very nicely shares her pizza, and when she asks if anyone will help her do the dishes, the duck, the dog, and the cat all say, "I will."

Teague, Mark
Dear Mrs. LaRue: Letters from Obedience School
Illustrated by the author. Scholastic, 2002

Ike LaRue, a dog, is sent by his owner, Gertrude LaRue, to the Igor Brotweiler Canine Academy, an obedience school. The dog sends a series of letters to his owner complaining about the terrible conditions. Black-and-white illustrations support his points. We see Ike in striped prison garb being dragged off to "Solitary Confinement" by two large guards. The accompanying color pictures, however, show the real story. We see Ike sitting at a table while the nice warden passes out dog treats. Another scene shows a black-and-white image of Ike begging for another bowl of gruel, à la Oliver Twist. In the corresponding color illustration, his menu shows the Brotweiler specialty—a "golden chewy bone with gravy."

Companion books: *Detective LaRue: Letters from the Investigation* (Scholastic, 2004); *LaRue for Mayor: Letters from the Campaign Trail* (Blue Sky, 2008); *LaRue across America: Postcards from the Vacation* (Blue Sky, 2011)

Thomas, Jan
Rhyming Dust Bunnies
Illustrated by the author. Atheneum, 2009

In what may be the silliest scratch-your-head-and-try-to-figure-out-where-this-idea-came-from picture book concept since Mo Willems's *Don't Let the Pigeon Drive the Bus!*, we follow four colorful specks of dust as they play rhyming games. Ed, Ned, Ted, and Bob talk directly to the reader. Ed, Ned, and Ted shout out words that rhyme, while Bob shouts out other words and phrases. We soon learn that Bob is warning the others about danger. When the other three dust bunnies rhyme "dog," Bob blurts out "Look out! Here comes a big scary monster with a broom!" Ned says, "Bob, no . . . 'Look out! Here comes a big scary monster with a broom!' does not rhyme with *anything*, really."

Companion book: *Here Comes the Big, Mean Dust Bunny!* (Beach Lane, 2009)

Trivizas, Eugene
The Three Little Wolves and the Big Bad Pig
Illustrated by Helen Oxenbury. Margaret K. McElderry, 1993

This is my favorite modern-day retelling of a traditional folktale. Three, fluffy, gentle wolves are told by their mother to go out into the world and build a house. "But beware of the big bad pig." The wolves buy bricks from a kangaroo and build a brick house. The big bad pig comes along and huffs and puffs, but "the house didn't fall down. But the pig wasn't called big and bad for nothing. He went and fetched his sledgehammer, and he knocked the house down." The wolves next build a house of concrete. The pig knocks it down with his pneumatic drill. The wolves then build a strong house with barbed wire, armor plates, heavy padlocks, and Plexiglas. The pig blows it up with dynamite. The wolves build a house made out of flowers. The pig huffs and puffs and inhales the fragrant scent. He turns into the big *good* pig and dances the tarantella.

Vernick, Audrey
Is Your Buffalo Ready for Kindergarten?
Illustrated by Daniel Jennewein. Balzer and Bray, 2010

A little girl brings her buffalo, complete with a backpack, to kindergarten with her. As young readers read about the buffalo, they also learn some basic rules of kindergarten, such as "cooperating" and "taking turns." The buffalo is likely to enjoy recess, but "He may need time to get used to the No Grazing rule." In art, "you never know what kind of masterpiece those hooves might create." The buffalo learns to share, but the other kids balk at snack time when the buffalo pulls out grass. "But he may be the only one who eats grass, then throws it up in his mouth and eats it again. Remember: Everyone's special in his or her own way."

Companion book: *Teach Your Buffalo to Play Drums* (Balzer and Bray, 2011)

Viorst, Judith
Alexander and the Terrible, Horrible, No Good, Very Bad Day
Illustrated by Ray Cruz. Atheneum, 1972

Right off the bat, Alexander "could tell it was going to be a terrible, horrible, no good, very bad day." He slept with gum in his hair and he trips on his skateboard as he gets out of bed. When his brothers get cool prizes in their cereal boxes and Alexander only finds cereal in his cereal box, he thinks about moving to Australia. Things don't improve at school. "Mrs. Dickens likes Paul's picture of the sailboat better than my picture of the invisible castle." After school, the dentist finds that Alexander has a cavity. The evening is no better: "There were lima beans for dinner and I hate limas. There was kissing on TV and I hate kissing." His mother tells him some days are rough, even in Australia.

Companion books: *Alexander, Who Used to Be Rich Last Sunday* (Atheneum, 1978); *Alexander, Who's Not (Do You Hear Me? I Mean It!) Going to Move* (Atheneum, 1995)

Waber, Bernard
Bearsie Bear and the Surprise Sleepover Party
Illustrated by the author. Houghton Mifflin, 1997

One cold night, Moosie Moose wanders over to Bearsie Bear's house and knocks at the door. "'It's me, Moosie Moose,' said Moosie Moose. 'Moosie Moose?' said Bearsie Bear. 'Yes, Moosie Moose,' said Moosie Moose." Bearsie Bear lets Moosie Moose jump into bed. The hilarious, alliterative sequence continues with Cowsie Cow, Piggie Pig, Foxie Fox, and Goosie Goose. When Porkie Porcupine jumps into bed, the other animals yell, "Ouch," and run outside. Bearsie Bear, who stays behind, informs Porkie Porcupine that he'll have to sleep by himself. Porkie Porcupine curls up under the bed, and the other animals show up at the door again. "Bearsie Bear opened the door and said, 'It's still cold outside and you want to come in again.' 'We were about to say that,' they answered." Eventually, Porkie Porcupine rejoins them in the bed and promises not to thrash about.

Waber, Bernard
Ira Sleeps Over
Illustrated by the author. Houghton Mifflin, 1972

Ira frets about taking his teddy bear to a sleepover. He's afraid that his friend Reggie will laugh and think Ira is a baby. Instead of reassuring her brother,

Ira's sister torments him. "'He won't laugh,' said my mother. 'He won't laugh,' said my father. 'He'll laugh,' said my sister." Ira meets with Reggie before the sleepover and they make plans. Ira tries to find out how Reggie feels about teddy bears, but he doesn't get a clear answer. Ira's sister continues to tease her brother. "And did you think about how he will laugh and say Tah Tah is a silly, baby name, even for a teddy bear?" During the sleepover, the boys scare themselves with ghost stories. Ira is happy to see Reggie grab a teddy bear. (Reggie's teddy bear's name is Foo Foo.)

Companion book: *Ira Says Goodbye* (Houghton Mifflin, 1988)

Waddell, Martin
Farmer Duck
Illustrated by Helen Oxenbury. Candlewick, 1992

A poor duck has the misfortune to work for a lazy farmer who spends the day in bed. As the duck does all of the chores, the farmer yells out, "How goes the work?" The duck replies, "Quack!" The duck serves the farmer meals in bed, fetches the cow from the field, carries the sheep from the hill, puts the hens in their house, saws wood, gardens, washes the dishes, and irons the clothes. The other animals take pity on the duck and make plans to help him. "'Moo!' said the cow. 'Baa!' said the sheep. 'Cluck!' said the hens. And *that* was the plan." The animals lift the bed with the sleeping farmer on it, throw him off, and chase him off the farm. Meanwhile, the duck is wondering why nobody is asking, "How goes the work?" The other animals tell the duck what has happened as they all pitch in to do the chores.

Walsh, Vivian, and J. Otto Seibold
Olive, the Other Reindeer
Illustrated by J. Otto Seibold. Chronicle, 1997

A dog named Olive mishears the lyrics to "Rudolph the Red-Nosed Reindeer." Instead of "All of the other reindeer," Olive hears "Olive, the Other Reindeer." She is inspired to show up at the North Pole. Santa Claus notices the dog lining up next to the reindeer and decides to give her a chance. The reindeer tie her up, and once they are in the air, Olive is shown dangling by a piece of ribbon. "Olive was surprised it was so easy to fly." When the reindeer crash into a tall tree, Olive helps by chewing the branches holding the sleigh. "Chewing sticks was something Olive could do well." Back up in the air, Olive notices first gumdrops and then flutes in the air. "That tree must have torn a hole in my sled." Once on the ground, Olive helps gather the flutes. "Olive was very good at fetching sticks." After all of the presents have been delivered, they fly into a dense fog near the North Pole. Olive uses her nose to guide them to Mrs. Claus's cookies. She earns her very own set of reindeer antlers. "They fit perfectly. Then everyone went outside to play reindeer games."

Watt, Mélanie
Scaredy Squirrel
Illustrated by the author. Kids Can, 2006

Scaredy Squirrel is afraid of leaving his tree. He's also afraid of "tarantulas, poison ivy, green Martians, killer bees, germs, and sharks." Scaredy Squirrel's emergency kit includes a can of sardines to distract the sharks if they attack. His daily routine is boring but safe. One day, thinking a killer bee is after him, he jumps from his tree. It turns out that he's a flying squirrel, and he creates a "new-and-improved daily routine" that includes jumping into the unknown. Check out the front endpaper, which includes a warning from Scaredy Squirrel that "everyone wash their hands with antibacterial soap before reading this book."

Companion books: *Scaredy Squirrel Makes a Friend* (Kids Can, 2007); *Scaredy Squirrel at the Beach* (Kids Can, 2008); *Scaredy Squirrel at Night* (Kids Can, 2009); *Scaredy Squirrel Has a Birthday Party* (Kids Can, 2011)

Watt, Mélanie
You're Finally Here!
Illustrated by the author. Hyperion, 2011

A rabbit addresses us directly and is obviously happy to see us. The rabbit's mood shifts back and forth. "Where were you?" he asks sternly. He tells us he's been waiting long enough for paint to dry, "long enough to learn an accordion solo." The rabbit acknowledges that perhaps we got off on the wrong foot and once again celebrates our arrival. But then he complains that it has been annoying waiting for us, "As annoying as a pet rock." The rabbit asks us to sign a contract that states, "YOU, the reader, hereby agree to stay with ME, the bunny (book character of *You're Finally Here!*), forever and ever." The rabbit's cell phone rings, and he turns his attention away from us. "Sure I'm free to talk—they can wait." He also says about us: "Yep, seems nice, no fleas, good steady page turner."

Why Did the Chicken Cross the Road?
Various illustrators. Dial, 2006

Fourteen children's book illustrators try to answer the age-old question through their pictures. Marla Frazee's explanation is that a sunny, grand building awaits the chicken on the other side—and as the chicken is leaving behind a rainy, dreary, gray chicken shack, she is thinking "Duh." Chris Sheban shows a guilty-looking chicken holding a baseball bat and looking at a broken window. Harry Bliss has the chicken escaping a horde of "mutated zombie chickens from Mars." Lynn Munsinger's answer is simple: "Because the light said 'Walk.'" The back section contains a "Scoop from the Coop," where the contributors respond to the question, "Why did the artist cross the road?"

Don't Let the Pigeon Drive the Bus! by Mo Willems

Wilcox, Leah
Falling for Rapunzel
Illustrated by Lydia Monks. Putnam, 2003

"Once upon a bad hair day, a prince rode up Rapunzel's way." He tries to rescue Rapunzel from her tower and calls up "Rapunzel, Rapunzel, throw down your hair." Unfortunately, she is hard of hearing. She thinks he said "underwear." A pair of pink panties lands on his head. She mistakes his words and tosses down dirty socks (instead of "curly locks"), a cantaloupe (when he asks for "a rope"), and a pig (a "swine") when he asks "how 'bout twine?" She also tosses down some pancake batter (instead of a ladder). When Rapunzel throws down her maid instead of her "braid," the exasperated prince decides to ride off with the cute servant. The maid tells him, "I fell for you when we first met."

Companion book: *Waking Beauty* (Putnam, 2008)

Willems, Mo
Don't Let the Pigeon Drive the Bus!
Illustrated by the author. Hyperion, 2003

A bus driver asks the reader to "watch things for me until I get back. Thanks. Oh, and remember: Don't Let the Pigeon Drive the Bus!" Pretty soon, a pigeon comes along and asks to drive the bus. The pigeon doesn't take no for an answer and employs a variety of tactics (and emotions) to change the reader's mind. "Vroom-Vroom Vroomy Vroom Vroom. Pigeon at the wheel!" The pigeon tries to influence the reader by proclaiming, "I have dreams, you know!" right before he (or she) explodes into a frenzied hissy fit. The driver returns and thanks the reader for not letting the pigeon drive the bus. The pigeon has new dreams when a big truck drives by.

Companion books: *The Pigeon Finds a Hot Dog!* (Hyperion, 2004); *Don't Let the Pigeon Stay Up Late!* (Hyperion, 2006); *The Pigeon Wants a Puppy!* (Hyperion, 2008). The pigeon also appears in a few board books.

Willems, Mo
Knuffle Bunny: A Cautionary Tale
Illustrated by the author. Hyperion, 2004

Daddy takes Trixie to the Laundromat. They accidentally put her stuffed bunny, which Trixie calls Knuffle Bunny, into one of the washing machines. Outside of the Laundromat, Trixie realizes that Knuffle Bunny is no longer with them. She has trouble communicating this fact to her father. When she yells, "Aggle flaggle klabble," he replies, "That's right. We're going home." Trixie fusses and goes "boneless" (her father has a hard time picking her up). However, once her mother is on the scene, the adults quickly realize that Knuffle Bunny is missing. They head back to the Laundromat. In one picture, they run past a man wearing a T-shirt featuring the main character from Willems's *Don't Let the Pigeon Drive the Bus!* When they pull the stuffed bunny out of a machine, Trixie yells "'KNUFFLE BUNNY!!!' And those were the first words Trixie ever said."

Companion books: *Knuffle Bunny Too: A Case of Mistaken Identity* (Hyperion, 2007); *Knuffle Bunny Free: An Unexpected Diversion* (Balzer and Bray, 2010)

Wood, Audrey
King Bidgood's in the Bathtub
Illustrated by Don Wood. Harcourt, 1985

The page at the castle cries for help. "King Bidgood's in the bathtub, and he won't get out! Oh, who knows what to do?" The knight says that they should battle and joins the king in the tub with miniature battleships and toy castles. He leaves, but the king still won't get out. The queen calls for lunch. She joins him in the tub, and they enjoy a huge feast that includes a tiny figure of the king in the bathtub on top of a huge cake. She leaves and the duke says it's time to fish. He climbs into the tub and suddenly it's filled with fish, turtles, and lily pads. Next, the court calls for a masquerade ball. Naturally, it's held in the bathtub. Finally, the page pulls the plug: "Glub, glub, glub."

The Silliest Easy Readers

2

Arnold, Tedd
Hi! Fly Guy
Illustrated by the author. Scholastic, 2005

A boy catches a fly named Fly Guy for the Amazing Pet Show. The boy is astounded that the fly is able to say the boy's name—Buzz. "You are the smartest pet in the world!" The judges laugh and say, "Flies can't be pets. Flies are pests!" Fly Guy shows the judges some fancy flying tricks, says his owner's name, and performs a diving act into his own jar. They award Fly Guy the Smartest Pet award. One funny visual is Buzz and his parents feeding Fly Guy by sticking an entire hot dog and bun (with mustard) in Fly Guy's jar.

There are eleven Fly Guy books. The second in the series is *Super Fly Guy* (Scholastic, 2006).

Caple, Kathy
Duck and Company
Illustrated by the author. Holiday House, 2007

Rat and Duck run a bookstore. When Cat comes in looking for a cookbook, Rat hides. "I'm looking for a book that tells how to cook rats." Duck successfully convinces Cat that a book about carrots is much better. While waiting for her chicks to hatch, Mother Hen turns down Duck's suggestion of the book "I Love You, My Dumplings" and instead buys a book titled "Terror Tales to Make Your Eyes Pop Out." Humorless Badger wants to buy a joke book and doesn't laugh at anything until Duck accidentally falls into a garbage can. Duck also performs a very successful story hour for "a stampede of little mice, frogs, rats, bunnies, and turtles."

Companion book: *Duck and Company Christmas* (Holiday House, 2011)

Minnie and Moo Go to the Moon by Denys Cazet

Catrow, David
Max Spaniel: Dinosaur Hunt
Illustrated by the author. Orchard, 2009

Max the dog dons his pith helmet, grabs his butterfly net, and goes looking for dinosaurs in his backyard. "A great hunter knows where to look." He declares that a football he finds in the flower bed is really a dinosaur head. A toy fire truck is a dinosaur's knee, a garden hose is a neck, a hockey stick is a jaw, and a tricycle makes up a dino's hips. Max gathers more things and begins to piece them together, to the amusement of a watching cat. However, once all of the pieces are put together, "the dinosaur comes alive," and the cat takes off in horror. At one point, the dog places a flower over his own mouth to simulate the dinosaur's lips. The illustration is a cross between funny and creepy.

Companion books: *Max Spaniel: Funny Lunch* (Orchard, 2010); *Max Spaniel: Best in Show* (Orchard, 2011)

Cazet, Denys
Minnie and Moo Go to the Moon
Illustrated by the author. Dorling Kindersley, 1998

Two cows—Minnie and Moo—want to drive the farmer's tractor. They believe the secret to turning it on lies in wearing the farmer's hat and repeating the magic words, "You broken-down, no-good, rusty bucket of bolts!" They lose control and the tractor crashes into the chicken coop, knocking the feathers off the hens. The tractor flies over a hill. When they land, Minnie and Moo are convinced they are on the moon. They don't recognize the chickens without their feathers and call them "moonsters." The chickens are mad and attack the two cows. Minnie and Moo get the tractor going again but land it in the pond. There is a marvelous illustration of one of the cows vaulting over a fence.

This is the first of more than fifteen Minnie and Moo books. The second in the series is *Minnie and Moo Go Dancing* (Dorling Kindersley, 1998).

Eastman, P. D.
Flap Your Wings
Illustrated by the author. Random House, 1969

A little boy is out for a walk when he finds an egg on the path. In the background, we see a body of water with alligators, turtles, frogs, and flamingos. The boy spots a nest high up in a tree, climbs up, and places the egg in it. Mr. and Mrs. Bird are surprised when they come home and see the egg. They feel it's their duty to keep it warm. They "wonder what kind of bird is going to come out of that egg." When an alligator hatches, they call it Junior and declare, "That's the funniest looking baby I ever saw." They try to keep up with the youngster's hunger by bringing it fruit, bugs, and worms. However, "Junior stops eating." The alligator soon becomes too big for the nest, and the Birds encourage it to fly away. "Jump into the air like this. Then flap your wings."

Griffiths, Andy
The Cat on the Mat Is Flat
Illustrated by Terry Denton. Feiwel and Friends, 2007

In the spirit of Dr. Seuss, Griffiths created nine silly stories that emphasize simple phonics and end rhymes. We meet Ed and Ted and Ted's dog Fred in one story (as well as a whale named Ned). There's also Harry Black who carries his snack in a sack. In the chapter titled "Duck in a Truck in the Muck," which features a duck named Chuck, Chuck gets his ice cream truck stuck in the muck ("what bad luck"). Buck shows up with his "brand-new shiny muck-sucking truck." Unfortunately, Buck's truck sucks up both Buck and Chuck

The Cat on the Mat Is Flat by Andy Griffiths

(as well as Chuck's truck). The book's thick chapter-book format will appeal to kids facing reading challenges who are slightly older than the typical easy reader audience.

Companion book: *The Big Fat Cow That Goes Kapow* (Feiwel and Friends, 2009)

Hoff, Syd
Sammy the Seal
Illustrated by the author. Harper, 1959
Sammy the seal tells the zookeeper that he would like to see what it's like outside the zoo. The zookeeper opens the gate and lets Sammy out. Sammy finds himself in the city. A lady asks him where he got his fur coat. "I was born with it." He follows a line of children going into a school. The teacher leads the children in song but stops them when she hears "one of you . . . barking—just

like a seal." She lets Sammy stay and he learns how to read and write. At recess, he catches a ball on his nose. "A boy on the other team tried to catch a ball on his nose, too." Sammy realizes the zoo is the best place for him, but he gets the children to promise to visit him.

Karlin, Nurit
The Fat Cat Sat on the Mat
Illustrated by the author. HarperCollins, 1996
This easy reader will challenge anyone with its tongue-twisting text. Wilma the witch has a flying broom, a fat cat, and a pet rat that she calls "my little brat." The rat hates the cat. The cat lies on a mat while Wilma the witch is out flying. The rat yells at the cat to get off. The cat won't, so the rat goes to get his bat. He comes back with a small winged mammal. A green hat with legs joins the rat and demands that the cat get off the mat. They all hear a "rat-a-tat" noise, and Wilma's broom flies in, knocking everything over. The rat, bat, and hat land on top of the cat on the mat. Wilma straightens everything out and they all leave. "'Thank goodness!' said the mat."

Kessler, Leonard
Old Turtle's Baseball Stories
Illustrated by the author. Greenwillow, 1982
In the summer, Old Turtle, Owl, Frog, Chicken, and Duck play baseball. In the winter, they huddle around a warm stove and tell each other baseball stories. Old Turtle tells the best story. He tells about the former baseball great Cleo Octopus, who threw "a fast ball, slow ball, curve ball, and knuckle ball" all at the same time. The umpire threw Cleo out of the game for this, and she quit baseball. She wound up working in a hot-dog stand, giving out hot dogs and collecting money at the same time. Old Turtle also tells the stories of Melvin Moose, who hit a double with his antlers; Carla Kangaroo, who played right field, center field, and left field at the same time; and Randy Squirrel, who stole bases by removing them from the park. Each time, Old Turtle is asked if the story is true. Each time, he replies, "Every word of it."
Companion book: *Old Turtle's Winter Games* (Greenwillow, 1983)

LeSieg, Theo
I Wish That I Had Duck Feet
Illustrated by B. Tobey. Random House, 1965
A boy uses his imagination to think of the advantages and disadvantages of having duck feet. "I wish that I had duck feet. And I can tell you why. You can splash around in duck feet. You don't have to keep them dry." You also don't have to wear shoes. His mother wouldn't like his duck feet in the house, however. So he imagines what it would be like to have two horns. "I could wear ten hats up there! Big Bill can just wear one." Unfortunately, he wouldn't fit through the school bus door. He goes on and imagines what it would be like to

have a whale spout, a long tail, and an elephant's nose. In the end, "I think that I just wish to be like ME." Fun trivia: "LeSieg" is "Geisel" spelled backward; Dr. Seuss's real name was Theodor Seuss Geisel.

Lobel, Arnold
Frog and Toad Are Friends
Illustrated by the author. Harper & Row, 1970

This volume contains five classic short, short stories about these two famous friends. "The Story" shows Toad trying to think of a story to tell Frog, who is sick in bed. However, he has trouble thinking of one. Toad paces, stands on his head, and dumps a glass of water on himself in an effort to think of a story. In the end, his crazy antics become the story. In the story "Spring," Frog tries to wake up Toad, crying out to him that it's spring. Toad refuses to get out of bed. He tells Frog to wait until "about half past May." Frog rips off the pages of the calendar until he gets to May. "Toad, Toad, wake up. It is May now." Toad is surprised and happily jumps out of bed.

Companion books: *Frog and Toad Together* (Harper & Row, 1972); *Frog and Toad All Year* (Harper & Row, 1976); *Days with Frog and Toad* (Harper & Row, 1979)

Lobel, Arnold
Grasshopper on the Road
Illustrated by the author. Harper & Row, 1978

Grasshopper has many encounters with insects and worms. The funniest is when he meets the "We Love Morning Club." He becomes a member but gets kicked out when he confesses he loves afternoons, too. The grasshopper moves on down the road and takes a bite out of an apple. A worm complains, "You have made a hole in my roof!" The apple rolls down a hill, causing the worm's bathtub to slide into the living room. The apple smashes against a tree. The grasshopper feels bad, but the worm says, "Oh, never mind. It was old and it had a big bite in it anyway." After many more episodes, the grasshopper goes to sleep. "He knew that in the morning the road would still be there, taking him on and on to wherever he wanted to go."

Lopshire, Robert
Put Me in the Zoo
Illustrated by the author. Random House, 1960

A spotted leopard wants to live in the zoo. The zookeepers carry him out. "We do not want you in the zoo. Out you go! Out! Out with you." Two kids ask the leopard why the zoo should let him stay there. The leopard shows them that he can change the color of his spots. "Look! Now all his spots are blue!" The leopard goes on to change the color of his spots to orange, green, violet, and multicolored. He is also able to put his spots on a wall, a ball, and a man's hat. He even puts some spots on the two kids. The leopard does many more amazing things with his spots. The children tell him, however, that he doesn't belong in the zoo. He belongs in the circus!

Companion book: *I Want to Be Somebody New!* (Random House, 1986)

Marshall, Edward
Fox on Wheels
Illustrated by James Marshall. Dial, 1983

Fox is upset because he has to take care of Louise when he'd rather be playing with his friends. While he's not looking, Louise climbs up a ladder and falls. He carries her up to her room and pampers her. She takes full advantage of the situation. When her friends ask if she can play, she hops out of her sickbed and runs outside. In the story "Fox and the Grapes," Fox is taunted by his friend Millie to join her high up in a tree. When he finally gets up, she tells him that she has no idea how to get down. Fox replies, "Well, that's just dandy!" Fun trivia: author Edward Marshall is really illustrator James Marshall.

Companion books: *Fox and His Friends* (Dial, 1982); *Fox at School* (Dial, 1983); *Fox All Week* (Dial, 1984); *Fox Be Nimble* (Dial, 1990); *Fox Outfoxed* (Dial, 1992); *Fox on Stage* (Dial, 1993)

McMullan, Kate
Pearl and Wagner: Two Good Friends
Illustrated by R. W. Alley. Dial, 2003

Pearl decides to make a robot for the school science fair. Wagner has many ideas, but never gets around to making anything. Pearl lets Wagner help make a "trash-eating robot." When a judge comes around, their robot falls apart. Wagner slips inside the robot and surprises the judge when she returns. When the judge approaches the robot for the second time, Wagner uses a robot voice to tell the judge, "YOU HAVE A NICE SMILE . . . AND SUCH PRETTY EYES." The judge is flattered, but when she opens the robot, we see the very tip of Wagner's nose peeking out. The two friends don't win a prize. Later on, after Wagner insults Pearl's green socks, he cleverly uses the robot to apologize.

Companion books: *Pearl and Wagner: Three Secrets* (Dial, 2004); *Pearl and Wagner: Four Eyes* (Dial, 2009); *Pearl and Wagner: One Funny Day* (Dial, 2009); *Pearl and Wagner: Five Days till Summer* (Dial, 2012)

Moser, Lisa
The Monster in the Backpack
Illustrated by Noah Z. Jones. Candlewick, 2006

Annie discovers a small monster in her new school backpack. When Annie first discovers the monster, he complains that she didn't knock before opening the backpack. When she wonders how she's supposed to do that, he replies, "Next time, ring the doorbell." The monster has eaten Annie's lunch, except for

Fox on Wheels by Edward Marshall

the carrots. "They make me burp." The monster wonders if he sleeps in Annie's boot, will "it give me boot-head?" Annie is worried when the monster rips up her homework, until she learns he did it to make confetti for "the Annie-Is-Great Parade."

Palmer, Helen
A Fish Out of Water
Illustrated by P. D. Eastman. Random House, 1961
A boy feeds his new pet goldfish a whole box of food, despite the warning from Mr. Carp, the pet store owner: "When you feed a fish, never feed him a lot. So much and no more, never more than a spot, or something might happen! You never know what." The boy names his fish Otto. Otto immediately outgrows the goldfish bowl, then a vase, various pots, a bathtub, a flooded cellar, and the city swimming pool. The boy calls Mr. Carp, who says, "So you fed him too much. I knew you would. I always say 'don't' but you boys always do." Mr. Carp dives into the pool and, after some nervous minutes go by, emerges with a normal-sized Otto. Fun trivia: Helen Palmer was Dr. Seuss's first wife.

Parish, Peggy
Amelia Bedelia
Illustrated by Fritz Siebel. Harper & Row, 1963
Amelia Bedelia's first day on the job has her dusting the furniture (by putting dust on the furniture), putting out the lights (which she accomplishes by gathering all of the light bulbs in the house and hanging them outside on the clothesline), and dressing the chicken (she makes an outfit for the evening meal's entrée). Luckily for her, she doesn't get fired for misinterpreting instructions because she makes a great lemon meringue pie.

There are eleven more Amelia Bedelia books written by Peggy Parish. The second in the series is *Thank You, Amelia Bedelia* (Harper & Row, 1964). After her death in 1988, Parish's nephew Herman Parish wrote several Amelia Bedelia books, starting with *Good Driving, Amelia Bedelia* (Greenwillow, 1995) and continuing through today.

Rylant, Cynthia
Mr. Putter and Tabby Pick the Pears
Illustrated by Arthur Howard. Harcourt, 1995
It is time to pick the pears. But Mr. Putter's cranky legs, cranky knees, and cranky feet are making it difficult. So Mr. Putter makes a slingshot out of his poodle underwear. "His brother had given him the underwear for his birthday. His brother loved the underwear. He thought it was funny. Mr. Putter did not." Mr. Putter uses it to shoot the apples that have already fallen on the ground at the pears on the nearby pear tree. He misses over and over. Mrs. Teaberry comes over the next day and says, "When I woke up this morning, there were dozens of apples in my front yard. And I don't even have an apple tree." Mr.

Putter is delighted to learn that Mrs. Teaberry has made "fourteen apple turnovers, five apple pies, six apple jellies, and a gallon of hot apple cider with cinnamon sticks."

This is one of many titles in the series featuring Mr. Putter and Tabby. The first book in the series is *Mr. Putter and Tabby Pour the Tea* (Harcourt, 1994).

Schwartz, Alvin
There Is a Carrot in My Ear and Other Noodle Tales
Illustrated by Karen Ann Weinhaus. Harper & Row, 1982

"A noodle is a silly person. This book is about a family of noodles." The Brown family has fun at the pool. They jump in, race, and bounce up and down on the diving board. A man comes by and tells them it will be nicer on Tuesday when there will be water in the pool. In another episode, Sam and Jane Brown are outside being bitten by mosquitoes. They put out the campfire and the mosquitoes stop. "They'll never find us in the dark." When some fireflies come by, the two kids run away, convinced that the mosquitoes have returned with flashlights.

Seuss, Dr.
The Cat in the Hat
Illustrated by the author. Random House, 1957

This is the book that started the whole easy reader genre. The world-famous cat who wears the world's most recognizable hat brings Thing One and Thing Two over to the house one boring, rainy day while Mother is away. The pet fish worries and says, "They should not be here when your mother is not! Put them out! Put them out! Said the fish in the pot." Thing One and Thing Two fly kites in the house. They knock things over and make a mess. With Mother approaching the house, the children catch Thing One and Thing Two. The cat takes them out but comes back with a machine that quickly cleans up the house. The kids wonder if they should tell their mother about their day. "What would you do if your mother asked YOU?"

Companion book: *The Cat in the Hat Comes Back!* (Random House, 1958)

Seuss, Dr.
Green Eggs and Ham
Illustrated by the author. Random House, 1960

Sam-I-Am tries to get another character to eat green eggs and ham. He asks, "Would you like them here or there?" He goes on to ask if the other character would like them in a house with a mouse, in a box with a fox, in a car and up a tree, on a train and in the dark and in the rain, and with a goat in a boat. The character constantly replies, "I do not like them here or there. I do not like them anywhere. I do not like green eggs and ham." He finally tries them and changes his tune: "I do so like green eggs and ham! Thank you! Thank you, Sam-I-Am!"

Seuss, Dr.
One Fish, Two Fish, Red Fish, Blue Fish
Illustrated by the author. Random House, 1960

Several short episodes introduce us to a variety of Seuss characters. We meet Mr. Gump, who rides a seven-hump Wump. "If you like to go Bump! Bump! just jump on the hump of the Wump of Gump." There is a character who cannot hear. It turns out he has a bird in his ear. There's someone called a Nook who has a cookbook he wears hanging from a hook on his hat. "But a Nook can't read, so a Nook can't cook. So . . . what good to a Nook is a hook cook book?" At the end of the book, we are told, "Today is gone, today was fun. Tomorrow is another one. Every day, from here to there, funny things are everywhere."

Sierra, Judy
Never Kick a Ghost and Other Silly Chillers
Illustrated by Pascale Constantin. HarperCollins, 2011

Tombstones in a cemetery feature silly epitaphs, such as "Here lies the body of Anna, our sister. She was just fine until Dracula kissed her." The final story— "The Big Slobbery Monster"—is the funniest. A boy is chased by a green slobbery monster who says, "Look what I can do with my long green fingers and my floppy purple lips." The boy screams and runs away. The monster follows and repeats its statement. The boy screams again and runs home. He locks himself in his bedroom, turns around, and finds the monster behind him. The monster repeats its line, puts its fingers to its lips, and goes "Blub-blub-a! Blub-blub-a! Blub-blub-a!"

Silverman, Erica
Cowgirl Kate and Cocoa
Illustrated by Betsy Lewin. Harcourt, 2005

Cowgirl Kate has several small adventures with her talking horse, Cocoa. In the first story, Cocoa doesn't want to wear horseshoes. We see him trying on cowboy boots instead. When Cowgirl Kate is upset about her rope twirling, she convinces Cocoa to pretend to be a cow. "I'm much too smart to be a cow." She tells him she'll provide pizza if he goes along with it. "'Okay,' he said. 'I'll be a cow. But I will not say moo.'" When the two friends play hide-and-seek, Cowgirl Kate hides and waits a long time for Cocoa to find her. She finds him in a cornfield, where he informs her that he likes his new game better. "It's called . . . hide-and-*eat*."

Companion books: *Cowgirl Kate and Cocoa: Partners* (Harcourt, 2006); *Cowgirl Kate and Cocoa: School Days* (Harcourt, 2007); *Cowgirl Kate and Cocoa: Rain or Shine* (Harcourt, 2008); *Cowgirl Kate and Cocoa: Horse in the House* (Harcourt, 2009); *Cowgirl Kate and Cocoa: Spring Babies* (Harcourt, 2010)

Thomas, Shelley Moore
Good Night, Good Knight
Illustrated by Jennifer Plecas. Dutton, 2000

While standing guard at the castle, the Good Knight hears a very loud roar coming from the forest. He jumps on his horse and investigates. "Clippety-clop. Clippety-clop." He finds a dragon, draws his sword, and then notices the dragon is wearing pajamas. The dragon asks for a glass of water and then climbs into bed. The Good Knight returns to the castle. He hears another roar and, "Clippety-clop. Clippety-clop," finds another dragon who asks for a bedtime story. The first dragon asks for another glass of water. This scenario is played out a third time when another dragon requests a bedtime song. When the Good Knight makes this last trip to the cave, the dragons want a goodnight kiss. They line up, eyes closed, lips puckered.

Companion books: *Get Well, Good Knight* (Dutton, 2002); *Happy Birthday, Good Knight* (Dutton, 2006). There are also picture books featuring the Good Knight and his friends: *Take Care, Good Knight* (Dutton, 2006); *A Cold Winter's Good Knight* (Dutton, 2008); *A Good Knight's Rest* (Dutton, 2011).

Underwood, Deborah
Pirate Mom
Illustrated by Stephen Gilpin. Random House, 2006

Pete's mother is hypnotized by the Amazing Marco. "When I clap my hands, you will be a pirate." Before he can bring her back, Marco is rushed to the hospital, where his wife is having a baby. Mom dons a scarf, an eye patch, and Pete's pet parrot and swishes "a wooden spoon at the mailman." "'Arrr!' said Pirate Mom. 'Arrrrrrgh!' said Pete." Pirate Mom picks a fight with a neighbor, calls another neighbor a bilge rat, and steals "underwear from Mrs. Burt's clothesline." After they catch up with the Amazing Marco, he switches Mom back to her normal self. Pete and his mother roll their eyes when Marco, as a form of apology, sends them two complimentary tickets to his next show.

Weeks, Sarah
Baa-Choo!
Illustrated by Jane Manning. HarperCollins, 2004

Sam the lamb tries to sneeze. "'Baa . . . ahhh . . .' No *choo.*" He protests, "this sneeze will never do" without the "*choo.*" Gwen the hen tries to help by tickling his nose with a feather. Sig the pig sprinkles pepper in front of an electric fan. Franny Nannygoat kicks up dust. Finally, all of the animals try all three tricks at once. "Sam the lamb let out a sneeze that raised the roof and shook the trees." The final illustration shows that Sam has blown the other characters up into a tree and onto a roof. They respond, "Bless you!"

Wiseman, Bernard
Morris the Moose
Illustrated by the author. Harper, 1959

Morris the Moose meets a cow and tries to convince her that she, too, is a moose. "'You have four legs and a tail and things on your head,' said Morris. 'You are a moose.'" The cow says that her mother was a cow. "Your mother must be a moose, too!" They ask a nearby deer to settle the debate. The deer tells them that they are both deer. All three ask a horse, who makes fun of their horns and antlers. "Let's ask somebody else. But first, let's get a drink." While looking at their reflections in the water, the three animals realize they don't look like each other. Morris says that he made "a MOOSEtake!"

There are several more books featuring Morris the Moose, as well as a series featuring Morris and his friend Boris. The second book in the Morris series is *Morris the Cowboy, a Policeman, and a Baby Sitter* (Harper & Row, 1960).

The Silliest Chapter Books

3

Anderson, M. T.
Jasper Dash and the Flame-Pits of Delaware
Illustrated by Kurt Cyrus. Beach Lane, 2009

Jasper and his two pals, Katie and Lily, live in a town so boring that it is fanatical about the school's Stare-Eyes team (opponents stare at each other and the first one to blink loses). After losing the championship, our heroes follow their opponents back to the mountains, jungles, dinosaurs, cannibals, and monsters of Delaware—yes, that Delaware. Jasper's evil archnemesis, Booby Spandrel, has taken over the lost monastery of Vbngoom, a special place for Jasper. The three heroes' humorous disagreements spur frequent laughs. When a dinosaur is chasing them, Jasper insists it's a Tyrannosaurus rex, while Katie remembers from her school report that it's an Allosaurus. Jasper: "While I respect your hypothesis—" Katie: "La la la la la! Not listening!"

Companion books. *Whales on Stilts* (Harcourt, 2005); *The Clue of the Linoleum Lederhosen* (Harcourt, 2006); *Agent Q, or The Smell of Danger* (Beach Lane, 2010); *Zombie Mommy* (Beach Lane, 2011).

Atwater, Richard, and Florence Atwater
Mr. Popper's Penguins
Illustrated by Robert Lawson. Little, Brown, 1938

When a penguin named Captain Cook arrives at Mr. Popper's house, Mr. Popper tries to find out "what the municipal ordinance about penguins is." He gets nowhere. When Mr. Popper takes Captain Cook on a neighborhood stroll, people refer to the penguin as a goose, a pelican, and a dodo. The penguin is sad until the Poppers purchase a second penguin—Greta. Soon Captain Cook and Greta have ten chicks: "They were Nelson, Columbus, Louisa, Jenny, Scott,

Magellan, Adelina, Isabella, Ferdinand, and Victoria." When the Poppers run out of money feeding the penguins and altering their house, they become a traveling show—Popper's Performing Penguins.

Auch, Mary Jane
I Was a Third Grade Spy
Illustrated by Herm Auch. Holiday House, 2001

When Brian's dog, Arful, learns how to talk to humans, Brian and his friends try hard not to let other humans know their secret. "If you tell people about it, they'll take him away from Brian so they can do testing on him." The boys do, however, take advantage of Arful's gift. They send him to spy on the girls to learn their secrets. Arful hears the word "dance," but when he reports his findings to the boys, he forgets the word. "'Well, there was something like ants. That's not the word, though.' 'Was it pants?' I asked. 'Plants? Slants?'" The boys figure the word was "France" and that the girls are going to make a soufflé. Later they decide to use Arful as a ventriloquist act for the school talent show. Arful turns out to have better jokes than the boys. "Why did the dog chase the cat? . . . To get a little catnip. Get it? The dog nips the cat?"

Companion books: *I Was a Third Grade Science Project* (Holiday House, 1998); *I Was a Third Grade Bodyguard* (Holiday House, 2003)

Avi
Romeo and Juliet—Together (and Alive!) at Last
Orchard, 1987

Eighth grader Pete Saltz has a crush on Anabell Stackpoole, but he won't tell her. His buddy, narrator Ed Sitrow, devises a plan to cast Saltz as Romeo and Anabell as Juliet in a quickly thrown together, student-driven production of Shakespeare's play. Sitrow soon finds himself in over his head. Saltz's rival Hamilton tries to sabotage the play, the spotlight girl has a crush on Sitrow (and doesn't know how to operate the spotlight), and the set and costumes aren't ready until the last possible moment. As a result, the play features everything from log cabins to pointy-toed shoes with jingling bells and crowns from Burger King. At one point, Sitrow looks up the definition of "love" in the dictionary. He informs some friends that Saltz is in love, hilariously repeating the dictionary definition: "He has an attraction, desire, or affection for her, too. And while I know it's hard to believe, she seems to be arousing delight, admiration, tenderness (of an elicit kind), sympathetic interest, as well as benevolence and devoted affection." In another episode, Saltz is worried about the play's kissing scene. He's never kissed a girl before. Neither has Sitrow, who instructs Saltz to scrunch and suck and practice on a Cabbage Patch Kid or the dog.

Badger, Meredith
Fairy School Dropout
Illustrated by Michelle Mackintosh. Feiwel and Friends, 2009

Elly Knottleweed-Eversprightly hates being a fairy. She prefers riding her skateboard to flying. She constantly forgets to use her magic wand properly. "They came with manuals that were as thick as the wands were high, and were about as easy to read as flying backward through a hailstorm." Elly has been kicked out of two fairy schools and is in danger of flunking out of her current one. "Out of four tests she'd had since arriving at Mossy Blossom, she'd failed five." (She failed the last test so badly that her teacher failed her twice.) She was kicked out of the first school for sticking her wand into a drinking fountain and causing a geyser of water to break through the ceiling "to the classroom above." The teacher in that classroom "was forced to bounce up and down on the jet [of water] until someone rescued her." Elly was expelled from the second school because she caught a "flyrus," which "is like a virus, except it affects wings and makes anyone who catches it fly backward." Unfortunately, Elly infected the entire school population. Finally, she gets caught in a human's house—a serious fairy offense.

Companion books: *Fairy School Dropout Undercover* (Feiwel and Friends, 2010); *Fairy School Dropout: Over the Rainbow* (Feiwel and Friends, 2011)

Barrows, Annie
Ivy and Bean and the Ghost That Had to Go
Illustrated by Sophie Blackall. Chronicle, 2006

Ivy is "the quietest kid in the class." Bean is the most rambunctious. The two get along fabulously. They take an oath to tell each other everything. They balk at the idea of a blood oath or a booger oath, and finally settle on a spit oath. Ivy makes up a story that a ghost lives in the school's girls' bathroom (to draw attention from the fact that she cannot do a cartwheel). Soon, all of the kids believe her story. Ivy and Bean decide to make a special potion to make the ghost go away. One of the ingredients the girls need for their potion is "the hair of an enemy." After a funny shouting exchange with her older sister Nancy, Bean sneaks into Nancy's bedroom and begins to "snip very, very quietly." The girls apply the solution, along with some special gifts for the ghost, causing the toilet to overflow.

Companion books: *Ivy and Bean* (Chronicle, 2006); *Ivy and Bean Break the Fossil Record* (Chronicle, 2007); *Ivy and Bean Take Care of the Babysitter* (Chronicle, 2008); *Ivy and Bean Bound to Be Bad* (Chronicle, 2008); *Ivy and Bean Doomed to Dance* (Chronicle, 2009); *Ivy and Bean: What's the Big Idea?* (Chronicle, 2010); *Ivy and Bean: No News Is Good News* (Chronicle, 2011)

Beaty, Andrea
Attack of the Fluffy Bunnies
Illustrated by Dan Santat. Amulet, 2010

Joules and Kevin's parents have sent the twins to Camp Whatsitooya on the shores of Lake Whatsosmelly. Their mother is excited that her children will be at Camp Whatsitooya. "'And they have a spa,' said Mrs. Rockman. 'See? There's even a picture!' 'It's an outhouse,' said Joules. 'It's rustic!' said her mother. 'What could be better?'" As it turns out, the camp owner and counselors have been replaced by three alien rabbits: "fierce, large, ugly, and ferocious furballs known as the Fierce, Large, Ugly, and Ferocious Furballs. (Fluffs for short . . .)" The kids must stop the rabbits from taking over the planet. Extra silliness creeps in when the author sometimes speaks directly to the reader. For example, she tells the reader to look at the chart at the end of chapter 7, and notes: "We'll amuse ourselves by singing while you read. La la la la la la . . ." (this continues for an entire paragraph).

Benton, Jim
Let's Pretend This Never Happened
Illustrated by the author. Scholastic, 2004

Jamie records events in what she calls her "Dumb Diary." She feels threatened by a pretty girl named Angeline and is also worried about what kind of nickname Mike Pinsetti will bestow on her. The first diary entries have a description of Jamie playing fetch with her pet beagle, Stinker, and driving him crazy with fake throws. "When I finally realized I hadn't thrown the ball yet, I had probably done it about a hundred and forty times. Stinker was a little cross-eyed and foamy . . ." Jamie's reference to Angeline as "Princess Turd of Turdsylvania" will get a laugh, as will her complaint about how she has to eat her mother's cooking or else hear a lecture about the "hungry children in Wheretheheckistan." Jamie tells her friend Isabella that her lip gloss is actually a roll-on deodorant. "Friends tell friends they're wearing antiperspirants on their mouths."

There are a dozen books in the series. The second title is *My Pants Are Haunted* (Scholastic, 2004).

Benton, Jim
Lunch Walks among Us
Illustrated by the author. Simon & Schuster, 2003

Franny K. Stein is a little girl who is a mad scientist, even though the rest of her family is normal. She keeps bats in her attic bedroom as well as "a whole bunch of crackling electrical gizmos that Franny had made all by herself," a tarantula cage, a snake house, and her flying piranhas. She makes an effort to become a normal girl so that she can fit in with her classmates. When a Pumpkin-Crab Monster kidnaps her teacher, Franny resorts to her namesake's talents and creates a Lunch-Meat Creature to save the day. At one point, Franny finds something growing in the classroom trash can. She asks her classmates what they have added to the can. She says, "That was close. Well, as long as NOBODY put any unstable industrial waste in there, we should be fine." Alas, one boy suddenly remembers that he "put some unstable industrial waste in there."

Companion books: *Attack of the 50-Ft. Cupid* (Simon & Schuster, 2004); *The Invisible Fran* (Simon & Schuster, 2004); *The Fran That Time Forgot* (Simon & Schuster, 2005); *Frantastic Voyage* (Simon & Schuster, 2006); *The Fran with Four Brains* (Simon & Schuster, 2006); *The Frandidate* (Simon & Schuster, 2008)

Birdseye, Tom
Attack of the Mutant Underwear
Holiday House, 2003

In Cody Lee Carson's diary entry for Wednesday, January 10, Cody's father is quoted as saying, "There are three kinds of people in this world: those who can count, and those who can't." Cody moves to a new school and is intent on being a "very cool New Me!" He declares that he is done finding himself in embarrassing situations. Unfortunately, while he's shopping for clothes with his mother, his new classmate Amy sees him in his underwear. She keeps quiet about it, and the two become friends. And then they become enemies. At the end, Cody saves another girl from a tipped-over Porta Potti—while wearing underwear all over his body, including on his head.

Blume, Judy
Superfudge
Dutton, 1980

Peter is upset that his parents have decided to have a baby (without consulting him) and move to New Jersey (again, without consulting him). He also has to deal with his little brother, Farley, aka Fudge. Among the many funny incidents that occur throughout the book, Fudge names his new pet myna bird Uncle Feather and his first kindergarten teacher Rat Face. In another hilarious episode, Peter has to pee really badly. "But Fudge was already in there, sitting on the toilet, turning the pages of *Arthur the Anteater*. 'Hurry up,' I told him. 'I've got to go.' 'It's not good for me to hurry,' Fudge said . . . I raced down the hall and relieved myself. Fudge watched. He was really impressed. 'I never saw so much at once,' he said. 'Thanks,' I told him."

Companion books: *Tales of a Fourth Grade Nothing* (Dutton, 1972); *Fudge-a-Mania* (Dutton, 1990) *Double Fudge* (Dutton, 2002)

Bolger, Kevin
Sir Fartsalot Hunts the Booger
Illustrated by Stephen Gilpin. Razorbill, 2008

A very old knight named Sir Fartsalot arrives at the castle in the Kingdom of Armpit. Young Prince Harry mischievously tells the knight about the terrifying Boogers. Not realizing that he is the victim of a joke, Sir Fartsalot prepares to do battle. "'Where might one find one of these Boogers?' 'Oh, you never know,' Harry said. 'Sometimes they can be right under your nose. So to speak.'" The prank backfires on Harry when his father, King Reginald the Not Very Realistic, sends his naughty son to accompany Sir Fartsalot. Along the way, they have many battles with ogres, rocs, giants—even a castle full of princesses. Harry grows to admire the courageous knight and regrets his poor behavior. In addition to frequent potty jokes, Bolger includes many witty puns and other examples of wordplay throughout the adventure.

Bond, Michael
A Bear Called Paddington
Illustrated by Peggy Fortnum. Houghton Mifflin, 1960

Mr. and Mrs. Brown encounter a small, polite bear in London's Paddington Station. He tells them he has come from Darkest Peru. Mrs. and Mrs. Brown find a note on the bear's suitcase that reads "Please look after this bear. Thank you." They do just that, naming the bear after the train station. Paddington becomes a part of the family, which includes the children, Judy and Jonathan, and the housekeeper, Mrs. Bird. Paddington has several small adventures, including taking a difficult bath, going shopping and winding up in the store's front window, helping Mr. Brown win a painting competition, attending a play and impressing the cranky lead actor, getting lost at the beach, and performing magic tricks that don't always work. On his first morning with the Browns, Paddington is served breakfast in bed. Judy and Mrs. Brown are impatient to take Paddington shopping, so the young bear puts his bacon in his travel case. They are followed by dogs. Paddington has trouble navigating the crowds and escalators in the Underground. He gets separated from his companions and runs into trouble with an inspector. Mrs. Brown and Judy come to the rescue. The inspector has other things on his mind. "Judging by the noise coming from the top of the escalator there was some sort of dog fight going on. It needed investigating."

There are more than twenty Paddington books, including some picture book adaptations. The second book in the series is *More about Paddington* (Houghton Mifflin, 1962).

Bowe, Julie
My Last Best Friend
Harcourt, 2007

Ida May is a fourth grader. "In fourth grade you start to smell funny. So you get your first stick of teen deodorant . . . You rub some on. After five tries you finally hit your armpit." Ida May is upset when her best friend Elizabeth moves away. Mean girl Jenna calls Ida May "I-duh" and mocks her in front of others. Ida May's first encounter with the new student, Stacey, sparks laughs as Ida May is caught with eight pieces of Choco-chunks in her mouth. The two girls slowly begin to hang out with each other in the school lunchroom. Ida May notices a boy shooting spit wads at them. Stacey walks up to the boy and asks, "You *like* me, don't you?" at the top of her voice. She throws her arm around the boy, making him turn red with embarrassment. Ida May wonders "how a person with six spitballs stuck in her hair can do something like that."

Companion books: *My New Best Friend* (Harcourt, 2008); *My Best Frenemy* (Dial, 2010); *My Forever Friends* (Dial, 2011); *My Extra Best Friend* (Dial, 2012)

Byars, Betsy
Me Tarzan
Illustrated by Bill Cigliano. HarperCollins, 2000

Dorothy surprises everyone by getting the role of Tarzan in the class play. She can deliver an amazing Tarzan yell. Dorothy tells her mother that she beat out her "enemy," Dwayne Wiggert, for the role of Tarzan. She sends a note to him that reads, "Me Tarzan, you Dwayne." Dorothy's yell is so great that it attracts real animals whenever she lets loose. At one point, the schoolyard is filled with "dogs and cats as well as seven horses from the Friendly Riding Academy. . . . Apparently there is also an iguana." Dorothy's yell even makes a small child wet his pants. Trouble looms when her yell attracts all of the animals from a nearby circus to the school play. "And then—and then there was a trumpeting sound, almost like an elephant." Have fun doing your own Tarzan yell while reading Dorothy's lines.

Cameron, Ann
The Stories Julian Tells
Illustrated by Ann Strugnell. Pantheon, 1981

Julian's father declares that he's going to make some special pudding. "It will taste like a whole raft of lemons. It will taste like a night on the sea." Julian and his brother, Huey, help their father. After cleaning up, Father goes to take a nap. "That pudding is for your mother. Leave the pudding alone!" Huey sneaks a taste anyway. Julian says, "Since you did it, I'll have a taste." They each take another lick. They also spill some on the floor. Later, when their father brings their mother into the kitchen, he hollers, "WHERE ARE MY BOYS?" He tells the boys there will be some beating and whipping and takes them to the kitchen. Father tells Huey it's time for his beating. He makes Huey beat some eggs. Father tells Julian it's time for his whipping. Julian whips the egg whites. When the second pudding is done, Mother takes a bite and says the pudding "tastes like a whole raft of lemons. This tastes like a night on the sea." The boys, however, decline to eat any more pudding. The other stories in this collection include "Catalog Cats," "Our Garden," "Because of Figs," "My Very Strange Teeth," and "Gloria Who Might Be My Best Friend."

Companion books: *More Stories Julian Tells* (Knopf, 1986); *Julian's Glorious Summer* (Random House, 1987); *Julian, Secret Agent* (Random House, 1988); *Julian, Dream Doctor* (Random House, 1990); *The Stories Huey Tells* (Knopf,

1995); *More Stories Huey Tells* (Farrar Straus Giroux, 1997); *Gloria's Way* (Farrar Straus Giroux, 2000); *Gloria Rising* (Farrar Straus Giroux, 2002); *Spunky Tells All* (Farrar Straus Giroux, 2011)

Catling, Patrick Skene
The Chocolate Touch
Illustrated by Mildred Coughlin McNutt. Morrow, 1952
A boy named John Midas (get it?) has one bad fault: "He was a pig about candy . . . and above all, chocolates." He comes across a strange coin and then notices a candy shop he has never seen before. He exchanges the coin for a box of chocolates. At home, he eats the lone chocolate inside the box. "It was the most chocolaty chocolate he had ever encountered." The next day, John is delighted when his toothpaste turns to chocolate. He eats the whole tube. His orange juice turns to chocolate. So do his eggs, bacon, and toast. John starts to worry at school when the water in the water fountain turns to chocolate. His pencil turns to chocolate and "he only succeeded in making a chocolate smear where he should have written 72." Dr. Cranium examines John and declares that the boy's "whole system seems to be so chocolatified that it chocolatifies everything it touches." John finally seeks help from the mysterious shopkeeper after he kisses his mother on the cheek and she turns to chocolate.

Cleary, Beverly
Henry Huggins
Illustrated by Louis Darling. Morrow, 1950
While buying an ice cream cone at the drugstore downtown, Henry spots a stray dog. He calls the dog Ribsy "because you're so thin," and decides to take the dog home. He hops on the city bus with Ribsy, but the bus driver kicks them off. "No animal can ride on a bus unless it's inside a box." From the clerk in the drugstore, Henry borrows a box with the words "Don't let them call you Baldy" written on it. Henry sets Ribsy in it and boards the next bus. The driver kicks them off, saying that the box must be sealed with holes punched in it. Finally, Henry borrows a big shopping bag and manages to smuggle Ribsy onto the next bus. Unfortunately, Ribsy breaks out and runs up and down the aisle. Henry and Ribsy wind up going home in a police car. This is the first in a series of mini-adventures for Henry that includes throwing another kid's football through the window of a speeding car and having a can of green paint fall on his head. "I'm going to have a green Christmas and a white Christmas at the same time. Won't Mom be surprised?"

Companion books: *Henry and Beezus* (Morrow, 1952); *Henry and Ribsy* (Morrow, 1954); *Henry and the Paper Route* (Morrow, 1957); *Henry and the Clubhouse* (Morrow, 1962); *Ribsy* (Morrow, 1964)

Cleary, Beverly
Ramona the Pest
Illustrated by Louis Darling. Morrow, 1968

Ramona Quimby shines in her first solo book, after appearing in the Henry Huggins series and with her sister in *Beezus and Ramona*. The first chapter, "Ramona's Great Day," is a classic. Ramona anxiously waits for a gift after her teacher instructs her to "sit here for the present." Ramona also learns a new song about "the dawnzer lee light," wonders how Mike Mulligan goes to the bathroom while digging a hole (in the picture book *Mike Mulligan and His Steam Shovel*), gets into trouble by grabbing Susan's "*boing-boing* curls," and makes the other kids giggle with her snoring noises during rest time.

Companion books: *Ramona the Brave* (Morrow, 1975); *Ramona and Her Father* (Morrow, 1977); *Ramona and Her Mother* (Morrow, 1979); *Ramona Quimby, Age 8* (Morrow, 1981); *Ramona Forever* (Morrow, 1984)

Clements, Andrew
Frindle
Illustrated by Brian Selznick. Simon & Schuster, 1996

Even though this book is a sensitive and touching tribute to teachers everywhere, it has its hilarious moments. Nick butts heads with his new fifth-grade teacher, Mrs. Granger, a no-nonsense instructor who everyone is sure has x-ray vision. When Nick tries the time-wasting tricks that have worked in the past with other teachers to make them forget to assign homework, Mrs. Granger outwits him and Nick winds up with an extra homework assignment. Later, Nick invents the term *frindle* to describe a pen. His campaign to make all of the other students use this word drives Mrs. Granger crazy. When the photographer comes to take the class picture, he asks everyone to say "cheese." Instead, they all yell, "Frindle!" Mrs. Granger is furious. She posts a note on the bulletin board. "Anyone who is heard using the word *frindle* instead of the word *pen* will stay after school and write this sentence one hundred times: I am writing this punishment with a pen."

Clements, Andrew
Jake Drake, Class Clown
Illustrated by Dolores Avendaño. Simon & Schuster, 2002

Jake decides he's going to be the class clown. He likes the attention. He practices knock-knock jokes on his sister and makes funny faces in the mirror. One day, Jake starts thinking about funny noises. He thinks about burps and swallows air while working in his spelling workbook. When his stern student teacher, Miss Bruce, asks if he's done, he says, "NOOOOOOOOOOOOOOOOOOOOOOOOOOOOOPE" and proclaims it "the longest, loudest burp of my life!" Another day, Miss Bruce has a spelling bee, but her strict interpretation of the rules frustrates the students; some have to sit down even when they know the correct spelling. Jake gets angry about the kids' humiliation. He stands up to spell mouse, "but something inside my head snapped. I looked right at Miss Bruce and in a high, squeaky voice I said, 'Mouse: m-i-c-k-e-y; mouse.'" When Miss Bruce says he didn't spell the right word, Jake replies in his best Mickey Mouse voice, "Heh-heh—well then, I guess I'm out." Was that a smile Jake saw on Miss Bruce's face?

Companion books: *Jake Drake, Know-It-All* (Simon & Schuster, 2001); *Jake Drake, Bully Buster* (Simon & Schuster, 2001); *Jake Drake, Teacher's Pet* (Simon & Schuster, 2001)

Coville, Bruce
Aliens Ate My Homework
Illustrated by Katherine Coville. Minstrel, 1993

Rod finds himself helping miniature aliens apprehend an interstellar criminal—the father of a classmate. The aliens call Rod's little siblings "larvae." (Rod himself calls them "Little Thing One and Little Thing Two after I read *The Cat in the Hat* to them.")They land their spacecraft in Rod's paper-mache mixture and eat his volcano science project. When his teacher asks him about his project, Rod of course responds, "Aliens ate my homework, Miss Maloney." The aliens eventually fly away, thanking Rod "on behalf of the galaxy for the assistance you have rendered to date." Unfortunately, fifteen minutes after it leaves, the spaceship returns to Rod's room. The aliens have found themselves in need of a vital part for the ship. "I think the technical word is *doohickey*. Either that or *thingummy*."

Companion books: *I Left My Sneakers in Dimension X* (Pocket, 1994); *The Search for Snout* (Pocket, 1995); *Aliens Stole My Body* (Pocket, 1998)

Curtis, Christopher Paul
Mr. Chickee's Funny Money
Wendy Lamb, 2005

Steven is given a quadrillion-dollar bill by his blind, elderly neighbor, Mr. Chickee. The bill has a picture of soul singer James Brown on it. Steven learns that this bill is real and there are only five in circulation. Treasury Agent Fondoo tries everything to retrieve the quadrillion-dollar bill. The book contains a mix of realism and fantasy, as when a dictionary seems to talk to Steven. When Steven checks out the copyright page, he reads, "You're not a librarian, what are you doing on this page?" Later on, the dictionary calls him "diminutive" and a "dunce" and closes with, "Don't take it personally, but I call 'em like I see 'em!"

Companion book: *Mr. Chickee's Messy Mission* (Wendy Lamb, 2007)

Dahl, Roald
The BFG
Illustrated by Quentin Blake. Farrar Straus Giroux, 1982

The Big Friendly Giant (BFG), who is actually a "titchy" runt of a giant compared to nine other giants, befriends a little girl named Sophie. Kids will enjoy passages such as: "'The bubbles in your tummy will be going *downwards* and that could have a far nastier result.' 'Why nasty?' asked the BFG, frowning. 'Because,' Sophie said, blushing a little, 'if they go down instead of up, they'll be coming out somewhere else with an even louder and ruder noise.' 'A whizzpopper!' cried the BFG, beaming at her. 'Us giants is making whizzpoppers all the time! Whizzpopping is a sign of happiness. It is music in our ears!'"

Dahl, Roald
Matilda
Illustrated by Quentin Blake. Viking, 1988
Matilda is a young genius—she is "*extra*-ordinary, and by that I mean sensitive and brilliant." Unfortunately, her parents are blind to this fact. "The parents looked upon Matilda in particular as nothing more than a scab." They call her a chatterbox when she demonstrates perfect speech at the age of one and a half; and when she asks for a book (after teaching herself to read at the age of three), her father suggests that she watch television. Matilda puts superglue in her father's hat after a nasty episode. The hat won't come off, so his wife cuts it off. "She had to chop the hair off right to the skin so that he finished up with a bald white ring round his head, like some sort of monk." When Matilda starts school, she encounters the meanest principal in the world—Miss Trunchbull. After the principal grabs a little girl by her pigtails and tosses her out of the schoolyard, someone shouts, "Well thrown, sir!"

Dahl, Roald
The Twits
Illustrated by Quentin Blake. Knopf, 1981
Mr. Twit is a mean, hairy-faced man who hasn't washed his bristly nail-brushy face for years. Mrs. Twit is just as horrid, with "a glass eye that was always looking the other way." They play nasty tricks on one another. One day, Mrs. Twit drops her glass eye into Mr. Twit's mug of beer to scare him. She laughs and taunts, "I've got eyes everywhere so you'd better be careful." To get back at his wife, Mr. Twit convinces her that she's shrinking and that she has to be "stretched." The Twits also own a family of monkeys, "Muggle-Wump and his wife and their two small children." The Twits insist the monkeys do everything upside down. The monkeys and several birds trick the Twits, who become convinced that they themselves are upside down.

Derby, Kenneth
The Top 10 Ways to Ruin the First Day of Fifth Grade
Holiday House, 2004
Tony Baloney dreams about appearing on David Letterman's *Late Show*. He entertains his friends with a variety of Stupid Human Tricks and Stupid Pet Tricks that usually backfire and land Tony in trouble. He shows his friend Mo one brilliant idea—jumping rope "on an open flushing toilet." Unfortunately,

Matilda by Roald Dahl

he gets his foot stuck in the toilet seconds before Mr. Gore finds them. "Some kids called him Mr. Gorilla behind his back. That was understandable because he kind of looked like one." Tony even crafts a list for David Letterman of "The Top 10 Signs Your Fifth Grade Teacher Is Having a Bad Day," including number 8: "During math, he insists that 8 + 9 = 89." Later, Tony brings his dog, Meatball, to class for Pet Week. Ridiculously, the dog winds up in an aquarium full of water.

DiCamillo, Kate
Mercy Watson to the Rescue
Illustrated by Chris Van Dusen. Candlewick, 2005

Mr. and Mrs. Watson own a pet pig named Mercy. Mercy loves buttered toast. Mrs. Watson loves making buttered toast for Mercy. They are both in bed having buttered toast dreams (while Mr. Watson is dreaming about driving a fast car) when they are all awakened by a "Boom" and a "Crack!" The bed is in danger of falling through the second floor. When Mercy hops off the bed and heads outside in search of food, the Watsons believe she is going out for help. Mercy shows up next door and startles the elderly Lincoln sisters. While Eugenia Lincoln is chasing Mercy, the fire department shows up. They hear the Watsons' cries and save the day. Mercy, of course, gets all the credit.

Companion books: *Mercy Watson Goes for a Ride* (Candlewick, 2006); *Mercy Watson Fights Crime* (Candlewick, 2006); *Mercy Watson: Princess in Disguise* (Candlewick, 2007); *Mercy Watson Thinks like a Pig* (Candlewick, 2008); *Mercy Watson: Something Wonky This Way Comes* (Candlewick, 2009)

Erickson, John R.
Hank the Cowdog
Illustrated by Gerald L. Holmes. Maverick, 1983

Hank the dog is the Head of Ranch Security. He brags about the goings-on at the ranch and his importance in the scheme of things—from barking at the coyotes (causing his human to fire a gun in his direction), to going to town and insulting the dog in the next pickup truck by "wetting" the tires. Hank is convinced that tracks found near a dead chicken belong to a raccoon. His nose confirms it. "This nose of mine don't lie. If it says coon, you better believe there's a coon at the end of them tracks." Hank finds the culprit and gets ready for action. "I sprang through the air and hit right in the middle of the biggest porcupine I ever saw." Things go downhill for Hank when he's accused of being the chicken murderer.

More than fifty Hank the Cowdog books have been published. The second in the series is *The Further Adventures of Hank the Cowdog* (Maverick, 1983).

Evans, Nate, and Paul Hindman
Humpty Dumpty Jr., Hardboiled Detective, in the Case of the Fiendish Flapjack Flop
Illustrated by Vince Evans and Nate Evans. Jabberwocky, 2008

Humpty Dumpty Jr. tries to solve the case of his missing friend Patty Cake, the owner of Pat-A-Cake Bakery. Puns are scattered throughout the story (Dumpty is a "good egg who always cracks the case") along with sight gags (a fraud claim for a "Muffet, Little Miss / Spider Bite Injury" is pinned to Dumpty's office wall). Dumpty and a kid named Rat enter the Crusty Crinkles headquarters to confront Mr. Crinkles. Crinkles calls for his Employee of the Month—Mr. Fum, an ogre. When Mr. Fum tries to harm Dumpty and Rat,

Dumpty taunts the ogre: "Fe! Fi! Fo! Funk! You are just a puny punk!" The ogre goes out the window of the skyscraper. Dumpty and Rat finally get a confession out of Crinkles, who wipes his nose on his sleeve. "'Y'know,' Rat whispered to me, 'I feel kinda sorry . . . for his *sleeve!*'"

Companion book: *Humpty Dumpty, Jr., Hardboiled Detective, in the Mystery of Merlin and the Gruesome Ghost* (Jabberwocky, 2008)

Fitzgerald, John D.
The Great Brain
Illustrated by Mercer Mayer. Dial, 1967

Seven-year-old John tells several stories about his ten-year-old brother, Tom, aka The Great Brain. The boys and their family live in Utah in 1896. Everyone is talking because the boys' father has ordered the town's first water closet for their home. Aunt Bertha is worried they'll all become laughingstocks. The Great Brain enlists his little brother to charge neighbor kids a penny to watch the local plumber dig a hole in the backyard for the cesspool. They will also "be served refreshments." When the water closet arrives, everyone in town comes to see it removed from the shipping crate. "This is the thing-a-mah-bob you sit on!" Once the water closet is installed, Tom advertises, "see the magic water closet that doesn't stink," until Mamma puts an end to that business venture.

Companion books: *More Adventures of the Great Brain* (Dial, 1969); *Me and My Little Brain* (Dial, 1971); *The Great Brain at the Academy* (Dial, 1972); *The Great Brain Reforms* (Dial, 1973); *The Return of the Great Brain* (Dial, 1974); *The Great Brain Does It Again* (Dial, 1975); *The Great Brain Is Back* (Dial, 1995)

Fleischman, Sid
McBroom's Wonderful One-Acre Farm
Illustrated by Quentin Blake. Greenwillow, 1992

Farmer McBroom tells the tale of how he, his wife, and their children—"Will *jillhesterchesterpeterpollytimtommarylarryandlittleclarinda*"—were swindled into buying an eighty-acre farm by Heck Jones. Unfortunately, they learned too late that the eighty acres were "one piled on the other, like griddle cakes." *Fortunately,* that one acre had "topsoil so rich it ought to be kept in a bank." Plant one seed in the ground, and it grew and was ready to be picked in just a few seconds. McBroom and his brood had to fight any weeds that fell on the farm—they grew fast, too. McBroom claims that it's all true. "Anything else you hear about McBroom's wonderful one-acre farm is an outright fib." This fun volume contains three out-of-print McBroom stories in one collection: "McBroom Tells the Truth," "McBroom and the Big Wind," and "McBroom's Ear."

Companion book: *Here Comes McBroom: Three More Tall Tales* (Greenwillow, 1992)

Fleming, Candace
The Fabled Fourth Graders of Aesop Elementary School
Schwartz & Wade, 2007

This year's fourth-grade class at Aesop Elementary is the naughtiest bunch of students ever. When Mr. Jupiter shows up to be their teacher, he quickly wins them over with his easygoing manner and air of worldly experience. He even accepts their unconventional answers to his questions (for example, "Who can give me the definition of *goblet*?" "A small turkey."). One funny scene follows fourth grader Calvin, who wishes school were as simple this year as it was for him in kindergarten, "where school was fun and easy." He is sent to the kindergarten room to be a student helper. The kindergartners give him a hard time because he doesn't know their little rules, such as sitting with pretzel legs. Whenever he complains, "But I'm a fourth grader," no one pays attention. Calvin especially dislikes swishing his bottom to a "gray squirrel" rhyme activity.

Companion book: *The Fabled Fifth Graders of Aesop Elementary School* (Schwartz & Wade, 2010)

Greenburg, Dan
Dude, Where's My Spaceship?
Illustrated by Macky Pamintuan. Random House, 2006

Three young aliens from the planet Loogl—Ploo, Lek, and Klatu—are out joyriding because "Klatu had just gotten his pilot's license" when they crash-land on Earth. Before the crash, Ploo sends an E.S.P. or "esp" message. "'Did you remember to turn on the anti-gravs, Klatu?' 'Of *course* I turned on the anti-gravs,' Klatu esped back. 'I am not *stupid*, Ploo.' When Ploo wasn't looking, Klatu reached over and turned on the anti-gravs." Ploo is taken to Area 51 (the secret military base near Roswell, New Mexico). Lek and Klatu disguise themselves as Earthlings and search for Ploo. A guard tells them they are in a top-secret area but points out where they can find the man in charge. "Major Paine is in that large building, right over there . . . the one where they keep the aliens." Ploo is rescued by Major Paine's young daughter Lily.

Companion books: *Lost in Las Vegas* (Random House, 2006); *Chilling with the Great Ones* (Random House, 2006); *Attack of the Evil Elvises* (Random House, 2007); *Lights, Camera—Liftoff!* (Random House, 2007); *Thrills, Spills, and Cosmic Chills* (Random House, 2008)

Griffiths, Andy
The Day My Butt Went Psycho
Scholastic, 2003

Griffiths's introductory warning instructs, "If you are a parent or a teacher or even if you're just over eighteen, put this book down now! You won't like it." Young Zack's butt leaves Zack and leads a revolution of butts against humans.

Zack is attacked by a squadron of flying butts. He's worried they'll gas him. He grabs a tennis racket and starts "thwacking" them. When two flying butts attack him from different directions, Zack ducks in time and "the butts collided with a thunderous sonic boom." Zack is next attacked by "a cluster butt." If the title doesn't give an indication of what the entire book is about, sample chapter titles, such as "Stenchgantor" and "Methane Madness," will.

Companion books: *Zombie Butts from Uranus!* (Scholastic, 2004); *Butt Wars! The Final Conflict* (Scholastic, 2005)

Gutman, Dan
Miss Daisy Is Crazy!
Illustrated by Jim Paillot. HarperCollins, 2004

Eight-year-old A. J. hates school. "If you ask me, kids can learn all we need to learn by watching TV." His teacher, Miss Daisy, informs him she hates school, too. She also doesn't seem to know anything. The kids suspect she's an impostor. After Miss Daisy slips in an arithmetic lesson while discussing football, A. J. says, "sometimes it's hard to tell if Miss Daisy is serious or not." Miss Daisy doesn't seem to be able to grasp even the simplest mathematical concepts. She keeps asking the students to explain them to her. When Principal Klutz drops by to visit the class, A. J. says he knows all about the principal's office. It's in a basement dungeon where they tie kids up and force them "to listen to their parents' old CDs for hours."

This is the first of more than twenty books in the My Weird School series. The second in the series is *Mr. Klutz Is Nuts!* (HarperCollins, 2004).

Hale, Bruce
The Chameleon Wore Chartreuse
Illustrated by the author. Harcourt, 2000

Chet Gecko is a private eye. "I go to fourth grade at Emerson Hicky Elementary. I'm a lizard." On the first day of school, Chet is asked to solve a mystery. Shirley Chameleon's brother, Billy, is missing. "Shirley shook her head and stood up. One tearful eye looked at me while her other eye watched a gnat flying above us. Chameleons do that." Chet's first clue is an excuse that Billy's mom supposedly wrote: "Pls xcuze Blly frm skool today. He iz sikk." Chet is anxious to get information from the principal's office, so he raises his hand. "Mr. Ratnose, can I go to the principal's office?" Mr. Ratnose says no. Chet does this two more times before Mr. Ratnose gets fed up. "*Absolutely not!* You've interrupted me for the last time! Take this note and go straight to the principal's office."

There are fifteen titles in the Chet Gecko series. The second book in the series is *The Mystery of Mr. Nice* (Harcourt, 2000).

Hale, Lucretia P.
The Peterkin Papers
New York Review Children's Collection, 2006

These wacky stories first appeared in a magazine in the 1860s. The Peterkin family has difficulty resolving simple everyday dilemmas, such as putting their too-tall Christmas tree into the parlor (they decide to raise the ceiling instead of cutting the tree). The family will probably remind folks of Amelia Bedelia and Polly Horvath's Pepin family—folks who have trouble figuring out the simplest things. Possibly the funniest story is "The Lady Who Put Salt in Her Coffee." "She told the lady from Philadelphia the whole story—how her mother had put salt in her coffee; how the chemist had been called . . . how they went for the little old herb-woman . . . The lady from Philadelphia listened very attentively, and then said, 'Why doesn't your mother make a fresh cup of coffee?' Elizabeth started with surprise . . . 'Why didn't we think of that?' . . . They all went back to their mother, and she had her cup of coffee."

Hornik, Laurie Miller
Zoo School
Illustrated by Debbie Tilley. Clarion, 2004

Fans of Louis Sachar's Wayside School books will appreciate this story of sixteen children who are attending the brand-new Zoo School. The children's classroom is between the Elephant Yard and the Seal Pool. Their tanklike desks are filled with tropical fish (and later on with squids, rodents, skunks, and other surprises). The teachers are actually zookeepers, and the principal, Ms. Font, has never been seen. Teaching methods at the school are unorthodox, and three inspectors are trying to decide if they should close the school or not. One teacher, Mr. Dapple, has assigned the children to figure out which flamingo has exactly 600 feathers. He realizes the birds have not been fed. While he is off looking for flamingo food, the children learn that these birds are pink because of their diet of shrimp. When two flamingos eat cheese popcorn and pretzels, they turn orange and brown. The kids spring into action before the inspectors come. One student is the CIC—Cherry Ices Carrier; another is the FOF—Friend of Flamingos. One girl wants to help, but she is the Squirrel Crossing Guard: "Ursula held up her hand and a squirrel stopped midleap." The students feed cherry ices to the flamingos to restore their color. "'That's funny,' said Mr. Dapple. 'They all seemed so hungry before. I wonder what happened.'"

Horvath, Polly
The Pepins and Their Problems
Illustrated by Marylin Hafner. Farrar Straus Giroux, 2004

The Pepin family and their neighbors face a series of seemingly insurmountable problems. Throughout the book, the author solicits solutions from the readers. While some of the situations seem plausible and easily solved by normal folks, there are several problems that defy belief. One day, the Pepins' talking cow gives lemonade instead of milk. This is a problem because the Pepins want to serve cheese cubes to their neighbor Mr. Bradshaw. They decide to put a pear on the plate with the lemonade squares to "trick the eyes." Unfortunately, there isn't a pear to be found. On another occasion, the Pepins find themselves on their roof. The ladder has fallen down. Their neighbors kick aside the ladder while trying to come up with ways to get the Pepins down safely.

Horvath, Polly
The Trolls
Farrar Straus Giroux, 1999

Mr. and Mrs. Anderson are forced to ask eccentric Aunt Sally to watch Melissa, Amanda, and Pee Wee after the children's regular sitter comes down with the bubonic plague. Aunt Sally is from Canada. She tells them about customs and the children ask her what it is. "It's a place where they open your suitcase and look at all your underwear." During one scene, Sally plays with her green beans while spinning a story about Uncle Edward and Great-uncle Louis, "who came for two weeks and stayed for six years." The children detest green beans. "Uh-uh, no beans." However, they find themselves captivated by Sally's playful uses of them. They start to crave the beans after seeing Sally knitting with them, making walrus tusks, and dropping them in her mouth like the clothespins-in-a-bottle game. "We need beans. We need many beans, now."

Howe, Deborah, and James Howe
Bunnicula: A Rabbit-Tale of Mystery
Illustrated by Alan Daniel. Atheneum, 1979

Harold, the family dog, narrates the story of Chester the cat and a newcomer to the family—a bunny. The kids in the household want to name the bunny before bedtime. Their mother suggests "Bun-Bun" and "Fluffy." In the end, she is the one who comes up with the best name. "He's a bunny and we found him at a Dracula movie, so let's call him Bunny-cula. Bunnicula!" When white vegetables, drained of their juice, appear in the house, Chester is convinced that Bunnicula is a vampire rabbit. The climax comes when Chester attempts to drive a piece of steak through the bunny's heart, instead of a wooden stake.

Companion books (all written by James Howe): *Howliday Inn* (Atheneum, 1982); *The Celery Stalks at Midnight* (Atheneum, 1983); *Nighty-Nightmare* (Atheneum, 1987); *Return to Howliday Inn* (Atheneum, 1992); *Bunnicula Strikes Again* (Atheneum, 1999); *Bunnicula Meets Edgar Allan Crow* (Atheneum, 2006). There are also a few picture books featuring the Bunnicula characters, as well as two offshoot series: Tales from the House of Bunnicula and Bunnicula and Friends.

Jenkins, Emily
Toys Go Out
Illustrated by Paul O. Zelinsky. Schwartz & Wade, 2006
Six stories follow the adventures of a little girl's toys. StingRay is a cloth toy that spouts facts that are anything but accurate. Lumphy is a toy buffalo and Plastic is a bouncing ball. Highlights include Plastic going to the beach and getting caught by a "possible shark" (a dog), and Lumphy trying to snuggle in bed with the girl and StingRay, but not being able to fall asleep. In the chapter titled "The Terrifying Bigness of the Washing Machine," Lumphy gets smeared with peanut butter. He hears the girl's father say, "Lumphy will have to be washed." StingRay goes on and on about the dark, dirty basement, so Lumphy hides. The girl eventually finds him and Lumphy meets the washing machine (who is named Frank). After his initial trip through the wash, Lumphy goes out of his way to get dirty so he can visit Frank again. These tales are reminiscent of A. A. Milne's Winnie the Pooh stories.

Companion books: *Toy Dance Party* (Schwartz & Wade, 2008); *Toys Come Home* (Schwartz & Wade, 2011)

Juster, Norton
The Phantom Tollbooth
Illustrated by Jules Feiffer. Random House, 1961
Milo feels that everything's a waste of time. Arriving home from school one day, he finds a surprise package with a note: "FOR MILO, WHO HAS PLENTY OF TIME." In the package, Milo finds a genuine turnpike tollbooth, some signs, assorted coins, a map, and a "book of rules and traffic regulations, which may not be bent or broken." There is also a note that says, "Results are not guaranteed, but if not perfectly satisfied, your wasted time will be refunded." He hops in a toy car and drives off on an incredible, imaginary journey to Dictionopolis and beyond. He meets Tock the watchdog, a normal-looking dog with "the body of a loudly ticking alarm clock." At the marketplace, Milo encounters a bee—the Spelling Bee. "Perhaps—p-e-r-h-a-p-s—you are under the misapprehension—m-i-s-a-p-p-r-e-h-e-n-s-i-o-n—that I am dangerous." Milo continues on to Digitopolis, the Mountains of Ignorance, and other destinations that help him learn the value of time.

Kent, Derek Taylor
Scary School
Illustrated by Scott M. Fischer. HarperCollins, 2011
Regular human and monster kids both attend Scary School. The scariest things in the school are the faculty and staff. These include Principal Headcrusher, Ms. Fang, Nurse Hairymoles, Mr. Spider-Eyes, Dr. Dragonbreath, and Mrs. T, among others. Dr. Dragonbreath is possibly the most dangerous instructor.

"At 8:00 a.m. on the first day, there were thirty kids in Dr. Dragonbreath's class. At 8:12 a.m. on the first day, there were only two kids in Dr. Dragonbreath's class." Dr. Dragonbreath, an actual dragon who has a PhD in dragon history and lore, has five strict rules. Any student who breaks a rule will be devoured. Most students fall afoul of the last rule: "RULE NUMBER FIVE. THIS IS THE FORBIDDEN RULE. NO STUDENT IS ALLOWED TO READ THIS SENTENCE." Fortunately, the students are regurgitated as young dragons, to which one student's father says, "Cool!" Principal Headcrusher is pleased to learn that her school has been invited to participate in "the Ghoul Games—the annual competition in various games between all the Scary schools on Earth." Unfortunately, there's also a new rule: the winners get to eat the losers. This is a very funny read-aloud; think of Louis Sachar's Wayside School series with monsters.

Kinney, Jeff
Diary of a Wimpy Kid
Illustrated by the author. Amulet, 2007
Greg Heffley keeps a journal of his experiences in sixth grade. The drawings Greg adds to the journal are as much fun as his insights. He says he didn't learn anything last year from sitting by "hot girls"; the illustration shows a girl asking him to pass a note that says, "Greg is a dork." When Greg's mother tells him to try out for the school musical, *The Wizard of Oz*, he is happy to get the part of a tree because "1) they don't have to sing and 2) they get to bean Dorothy with apples." Greg dislikes Patty Farrell, the girl who plays Dorothy. Greg and the other trees forget their lines, notice an angry Patty Farrell, and start pelting her with apples.

Companion books: *Diary of a Wimpy Kid: Rodrick Rules* (Amulet, 2008); *Diary of a Wimpy Kid: The Last Straw* (Amulet, 2009); *Diary of a Wimpy Kid: Dog Days* (Amulet, 2009); *Diary of a Wimpy Kid: The Ugly Truth* (Amulet, 2010); *Diary of a Wimpy Kid: Cabin Fever* (Amulet, 2011)

Klise, Kate
Dying to Meet You
Illustrated by M. Sarah Klise. Harcourt, 2009
A famous but cranky children's book author, Ignatius B. Grumply, rents an old Victorian mansion in which to write his first book in twenty years. He is not a fan of his young audience. "I happen to write books for children. That doesn't mean I want to see or hear the little monsters when I'm trying to work." Imagine his dismay upon discovering that instead of a nice, quiet house, he has moved into a home already occupied by an eleven-year-old boy and a cat. Ignatius had failed to notice that this arrangement was stipulated in the contract. The ghost of an unpublished author also lives in the house. The cast of characters is fun to read: there's Anita Sale, the realtor; E. Gadds, a lawyer; Paige Turner, a

Diary of a Wimpy Kid by Jeff Kinney

publisher; Les and Diane Hope, two paranormal experts; Seymour Hope, their son; Frank N. Beans, a private investigator; Olive C. Spence, a ghost; and the editor of the newspaper—Cliff Hanger.

Companion books: *Over My Dead Body* (Harcourt, 2009); *Till Death Do Us Bark* (Harcourt, 2011)

Korman, Gordon
No More Dead Dogs
Hyperion, 2000

Eighth grader Wallace Wallace is the school's football hero. Normally a bench warmer, he got lucky and fell on a ball that won the county championship. He is proud of the fact that he always tells the truth. In his book report, he describes *Old Shep, My Pal* as "the most boring book I've ever read in my entire life." He also complains that the dog always dies. "Go to the library and pick out a book with an award sticker and a dog on the cover. Trust me, that dog is going down." Unfortunately, *Old Shep, My Pal* is his teacher's favorite book. Mr. Fogelman makes Wallace Wallace serve detention by missing football practice and attending rehearsals of the school drama club's production of— you guessed it—*Old Shep, My Pal*.

Krieg, Jim
Griff Carver, Hallway Patrol
Razorbill, 2010

Imagine a famous crime fighter from the 1940s, such as Sam Spade or Philip Marlowe, in the body of a seventh-grade member of the Rampart Middle School Patrol Squad. Young Griff Carver takes his job seriously. When he patrols the halls of his new school for the first time, he manages to catch the school principal littering. When called a hero, Carver responds, "A hero's just a sandwich the cafeteria served us every Wednesday . . . It was mostly bologna." Carver is suspicious about the school's most popular student, Marcus Volger. When told every kid in school likes Volger, Carver replies, "Every dog in the world likes to drink antifreeze, too . . . Too bad it's poison." With the help of his partner, Tommy Rodriguez, the ultimate scout who has earned merit badges in just about everything, Carver uncovers a fake hall pass operation.

Lieb, Josh
I Am a Genius of Unspeakable Evil
and I Want to Be Your Class President
Razorbill, 2009

Twelve-year-old Oliver Watson is secretly one of the world's richest master-minds; he just happens to attend seventh grade and live with his parents. His classmates look down on him and don't realize he has unseen bodyguards who punish any would-be bullies. He has the technology to type messages on his English teacher's cigarettes, just to mess with his head. When one popular boy gets on Oliver's bad side, the boy is forced to drop out of a school election when presented with pictures of him eating his boogers. However, a girl named Liz is not intimidated. In fact, she thinks the blackmail photos of her dancing in her pajamas and singing into a hairbrush are wonderful. "Can I get more?"

Lindgren, Astrid
Pippi Longstocking
Illustrated by Louis S. Glanzman. Viking, 1950

Pippi is an extraordinary girl who has remarkable strength. "Why, she could lift a whole horse if she wanted to! And she wanted to." Pippi lives with her horse and a monkey at her home, Villa Villekulla. Her neighbors Tommy and Annika meet her while she's walking backward. Pippi plays "tag" with two policemen who come to take her to a children's home. She climbs to the chimney of her house. When the policemen climb up a ladder to grab her, she jumps down and takes away the ladder. Later, when they pounce on her, she lifts them up and carries them "down the garden path, out through the gate, and onto the street . . . it was quite some time before they were ready to get up again." The police run back to town and tell the other adults that Pippi "wasn't quite fit for a children's home." Pippi also has encounters with a teacher, a circus ringmaster, and two burglars.

Companion books: *Pippi Goes on Board* (Viking, 1957); *Pippi in the South Seas* (Viking, 1959)

Lowry, Lois
All about Sam
Illustrated by Diane deGroat. Houghton Mifflin, 1988

This first book in the series that features Anastasia Krupnik's younger brother begins with the newborn Sam. He isn't able to make his family understand him. "I hate this hat," he yells, but his family only hears "Waaahhh." When he's old enough to go to school, he brings his father's pipe and lighter for show-and-tell. "'HOLD IT!' said Mrs. Bennett in a loud voice. 'Stop right there, Sam Krupnik. What on earth are you doing?' That was a strange question, Sam thought. Anybody could *see* he was lighting a pipe." He tells the teacher that the pipe is his and his father has a different pipe. "We sit around and smoke our pipes together at home . . . And my mom and my sister, they both smoke big cigars."

Companion books: *Attaboy, Sam!* (Houghton Mifflin, 1992); *See You Around, Sam!* (Houghton Mifflin, 1996); *Zooman Sam* (Houghton Mifflin, 1999)

Lowry, Lois
Gooney Bird Greene
Illustrated by Middy Thomas. Houghton Mifflin, 2002

Gooney Bird Greene is the new second-grade student in Mrs. Pidgeon's class. Gooney Bird "likes to be right smack dab in the middle of everything." She regales her teacher and classmates with what seem like tall tales, but Gooney Bird says, "I tell only absolutely true stories." Each story does indeed turn out to be true, although not in the way most of her classmates (and we, the readers) expect. For example, when Gooney Bird is late, her excuse is that she had to direct an orchestra. "Mrs. Pidgeon smiled. 'I hear all sorts of interesting excuses for tardiness, but I have never heard that one before.'" It turns out that a bus carrying members of a concert symphony band was lost and looking for the concert hall. Gooney Bird directed them to the hall, thus "directing the orchestra."

Companion books: *Gooney Bird and the Room Mother* (Houghton Mifflin, 2005); *Gooney the Fabulous* (Houghton Mifflin, 2007); *Gooney Bird Is So Absurd* (Houghton Mifflin, 2009); *Gooney Bird on the Map* (Houghton Mifflin, 2011)

Lowry, Lois
The Willoughbys
Illustrated by the author. Houghton Mifflin, 2008
The Willoughby children—Timothy, the twins A and B, and Jane—decide to become orphans and plot to send their parents on a sea voyage. At the same time, their parents are devising a plan for getting rid of the children. The children get a new nanny, who joins them in their effort to deter potential buyers of their home. They also acquire a new baby (found on their doorstep) whom they, in turn, deliver to a wealthy neighbor who is depressed because he lost his wife and son years ago. A fun example of the humor in this book is when a woman is convinced her son knows German. In truth, the boy simply uses "English words and added extra syllables with a vaguely Germanic sound. 'Helloschlimhofen,' the little boy said cheerfully. 'Neisch day, isn't itzenschlitz?'"

Lubar, David
Invasion of the Road Weenies
and Other Warped and Creepy Tales
Starscape, 2005
Lubar has written thirty-five short tales that are similar to the *Twilight Zone* and Stephen King's short stories, but for a younger audience. A few of the humorous stories include "Baby Talk" and "Bed Tings." In "Baby Talk," a girl learns that her baby brother can actually talk like a grown-up. They keep it their little secret, with the baby calling the shots. The girl soon realizes with horror that the family cat, dog, and goldfish also have the ability to talk. "Bed Tings" relies on bad puns. When a friend's grandmother tells the narrator, "Bed tings happen en treeze," he is relieved when a third bad thing happens to him and thinks, "I'm safe now." But when he later falls out of a tree and breaks a leg, he realizes that his friend's grandmother actually said, "Bad things happen in trees."

Companion books: *In the Land of the Lawn Weenies and Other Misadventures* (Starscape, 2003); *The Curse of the Campfire Weenies and Other Warped and Creepy Tales* (Starscape, 2007); *The Battle of the Red Hot Pepper Weenies and Other Warped and Creepy Tales* (Starscape, 2009); *Attack of the Vampire Weenies and Other Warped and Creepy Tales* (Starscape, 2011)

MacDonald, Betty
Mrs. Piggle-Wiggle
Illustrated by Richard Bennett. Lippincott, 1947
Mrs. Piggle-Wiggle is a small woman who lives in an upside-down house. And while she's nervous around grown-ups, "she knows everything there is to know about children," including how to correct bad behavior. My favorite is the wonderful chapter titled "The Radish Cure." Patsy decides one day that she doesn't want to take a bath. "I won't take a bath! I won't ever take a bath! I hate baths! I HATE BATHS! I haaaaaaaaaaaaaaate baaaaaaaaaaaaths!" Her mother calls Mrs. Piggle-Wiggle, who tells her to buy radish seeds. "The small

red round ones are the best, and don't get that long white icicle type." Patsy is to get her way and be allowed to become dirty. By the end of the third week, Patsy has a "layer of topsoil on her face, neck and arms." Her parents plant the radish seeds in the dirt that has accumulated on Patsy. A few days later, Patsy is horrified to find radishes growing on her. She breaks down and spends the entire day in the shower, using up two bars of soap. When her father comes home that evening, Patsy proudly holds out a plate of radishes.

Companion books: *Mrs. Piggle-Wiggle's Magic* (Lippincott, 1949); *Mrs. Piggle-Wiggle's Farm* (Lippincott, 1954); *Hello, Mrs. Piggle-Wiggle* (Lippincott, 1957); *Happy Birthday, Mrs. Piggle-Wiggle* (HarperCollins, 2007). This final book was cowritten by Betty MacDonald's daughter based on her notes.

Maguire, Gregory
Leaping Beauty and Other Animal Fairy Tales
Illustrated by Chris L. Demarest. HarperCollins, 2004

The author of the popular book and Broadway play *Wicked* wrote a fractured fairy-tale collection featuring stories such as "Goldiefox and the Three Chickens," "Hamster and Gerbil," "So What and the Seven Giraffes," "Little Red Robin Hood," "The Three Little Penguins and the Big Bad Walrus," "Cinder-Elephant," and "Rumplesnakeskin." One of the funniest stories is "Cinder-Elephant." When Cinder-Elephant mentions that she wants to go to the prince's ball, her stepmother replies, "The only ball you'll ever go to is the one you'll balance on when I sell you to the circus!" Of course, she goes to the ball—wearing two glass pie plates as slippers. After she runs away from the prince, he goes all over the kingdom to "find the one whose foot fit into a glass pie plate." Afterward, Cinder-Elephant's nearly blind father accidentally drives a bus over the feet of his former wife and those of her daughters. "At last their feet really *did* fit in glass pie plates."

Manes, Stephen
Be a Perfect Person in Just Three Days!
Illustrated by Tom Huffman. Clarion, 1982

While looking for a monster book in the library, Milo finds a different type of book. Or maybe it found him, as it "tumbled down from the top shelf and hit him on the head . . . The front cover screamed *Be a Perfect Person in Just Three Days!*" The instructions in the book tell Milo not to sneak a peek at the last page. Milo does, of course. The last page has writing on it: "BOY, ARE YOU DUMB! Didn't I tell you not to look at the last page of this book?" Milo takes the book home and follows the author's advice. Soon, Milo finds himself walking around with a stalk of broccoli around his neck per the book's instructions. Next, he has to go an entire day without eating. On the last day, Milo has to do nothing. "Sit! Think. Relax. Be like broccoli." After accomplishing all of this, Milo's in for a surprise when he comes to the end of the book.

Marshall, James
Rats on the Roof and Other Stories
Illustrated by the author. Dial, 1991
Marshall has written seven funny stories featuring an array of strange and quirky animals, such as Cedric Mousejoy and his bride Mary Louise Mousewood, cows, swans, frogs, and even a brontosaurus. In the title story, Otis and Sophie Dog learn that they have rats on the roof. (The rats dance and play musical instruments.) Otis and Sophie advertise for help and a tomcat shows up. The cat demands three square meals a day "plus snacks in the afternoon" and the sofa to lie down on. He also wants to be paid ten dollars a week. The cat is horrified to learn that the Dogs want him to help them with their rat problem. He knocks over furniture, bangs the piano, and screams out the windows before crashing through the screen door and running off down the street. "That night the Dogs were surprised to find a handwritten note on their bedside table." The rats were complaining about the noise disturbing their daytime sleep: "We find ourselves no longer able to remain in residence. We are leaving."

Companion book: *Rats on the Range and Other Stories* (Dial, 1993)

McDonald, Megan
Judy Moody
Illustrated by Peter H. Reynolds. Candlewick, 2000
Judy is in a foul mood her first day of third grade. When her teacher asks her if she's in a bad mood, Judy replies, "ROAR." Her mood improves when she and her classmates create "Me" collages. The project includes describing their favorite pets and the funniest things that ever happened to them. Judy buys a Venus flytrap and counts that as her pet. She tricks her brother, Stink, by placing a fake human hand in the toilet. In the chapter titled "The T.P. Club," Judy and her friends catch a toad. While she's holding it, she feels something warm and wet. "That toad peed on me." When the same thing happens to Judy's friend Rocky, they start a new club—the Toad Pee Club. Stink learns about their secret club. Judy and Rocky make Stink hold the toad. Nothing happens. "Oh well. Put the toad back. You can't be in the club." Stink suddenly feels something warm and wet on his hand. He's allowed in the club.

There are more than a dozen Judy Moody books. The second in the series is *Judy Moody Gets Famous* (Candlewick, 2001).

McDonald, Megan
Judy Moody and Stink:
The Mad, Mad, Mad, Mad Treasure Hunt
Illustrated by Peter H. Reynolds. Candlewick, 2009
Judy Moody and her brother, Stink, visit "Artichoke Island," aka Ocracoke Island, and get involved in a pirate treasure hunt contest. First prize is a gold doubloon and a ride on the *Queen Anne's Revenge Two*. As Judy, Stink, their parents, and other tourists are on a boat heading for the island, Stink feels sick.

The two kids go back and forth with "puke" comments. Judy makes a groaner of a joke, asking, "What do you call pirate throw-up?" The answer is "Pieces-o'-Ate!" Judy next instructs Stink to stick out his tongue and say "ARRRR." The two then start arguing about girls being pirates. Judy points out that there were famous female pirates like Anne Bonny and Mary Read. The book contains several clues and secret codes to decipher. "Toys Arrr Us" and "Marrrs Barrr Crunch" are two of the many pirate puns scattered throughout the text that will amuse young readers.

Companion book: *Judy Moody and Stink: The Holly Joliday* (Candlewick, 2007)

McDonald, Megan
Stink: The Incredible Shrinking Kid
Illustrated by Peter H. Reynolds. Candlewick, 2005

Judy Moody's younger brother stars in his first book. James Moody, aka Stink, is the shortest kid in second grade. "Shrimp-o! Runstville! Shorty Pants!" He frets about his height, especially after his sister measures him before bedtime and informs Stink that he's one-quarter inch shorter than he was in the morning. In the chapter titled "Shrink, Shrank, Shrunk," Stink's hair turns orange after Judy applies hair gel to make him appear taller. "'I look like a carrot!' said Stink. 'Carrots are tall,' said Judy." Once he arrives at school, Stink's classmate Elizabeth informs him that she prefers to be addressed as "Sophie of the Elves." When she tells him that to an elf, he would be a giant, Stink says, "Thanks, Sophie of the Elves."

Companion books: *Stink and the Incredible Super-Galactic Jawbreaker* (Candlewick, 2006); *Stink and the World's Worst Super-Stinky Sneakers* (Candlewick, 2007); *Stink and the Great Guinea Pig Express* (Candlewick, 2008); *Stink-o-pedia: Super Stink-y Stuff from A to Zzzzz* (Candlewick, 2009); *Stink: Solar System Superhero* (Candlewick, 2010); *Stink-o-pedia, Volume 2: More Stink-y Stuff from A to Z* (Candlewick, 2010); *Stink and the Ultimate Thumb-Wrestling Smackdown* (Candlewick, 2011)

McMullan, Kate
School! Adventures at the Harvey N. Trouble Elementary School
Illustrated by George Booth. Feiwel and Friends, 2010

Fans of Abbott and Costello's routine "Who's on First?" may enjoy the pun-filled adventures that take place during one week at Harvey N. Trouble Elementary School. The characters include a school bus driver named Mr. Stuckinaditch who constantly gets the bus stuck in a ditch, and Mr. Hugh da Mann, the kindergarten teacher. When the speedy boy Ron Faster gets to school, he finds his regular teacher, Mrs. Petzgalore, absent. The substitute, Mr. Norman Don't-know, doesn't know where she is (or much of anything else). The class roll call features, among others, Anita Dawg, Izzy Normal, Viola Fuss, and Gladys

Friday. It happens to be Abby Birthday's birthday. There's a mess and the two janitors—Janitor Iquit and Assistant Janitor Quitoo—quit. This all happens on a "hotsy-totsy Monday."

Milne, A. A.
Winnie-the-Pooh
Illustrated by E. H. Shepard. Dutton, 1926
Pooh lives in the Hundred Acre Wood with his friends Christopher Robin, Rabbit, Piglet, Eeyore, Owl, Kanga, and Roo. Some of their adventures include "Pooh and Piglet Go Hunting and Nearly Catch a Woozle," "Piglet Meets a Heffalump," and "Eeyore Loses a Tail and Pooh Finds One." One of the most popular chapters is "Pooh Goes Visiting and Gets into a Tight Place." After his Stoutness Exercises, Pooh visits his friend Rabbit. The two have a humorous exchange before Rabbit invites Pooh inside. Pooh eats quite a bit of food, and as he is exiting through Rabbit's front door, he gets stuck. "'It all comes,' said Pooh crossly, 'of not having front doors big enough.'" Christopher Robin shows up and announces that Pooh will have to wait a week to get thin. Rabbit uses Pooh's back legs as a "towel-horse" to hang his washing on, and Christopher Robin reads "a Sustaining Book, such as would help and comfort a Wedged Bear in Great Tightness." After a week and with the help of several woodland animals, Pooh's friends manage to pull him out: "'*Pop!*' just as if a cork were coming out of a bottle."

Companion book: *The House at Pooh Corner* (Dutton, 1928)

Nolan, Lucy
Smarter Than Squirrels
Illustrated by Mike Reed. Marshall Cavendish, 2004
Down Girl is a dog who lives with her master, Rruff, and next door to her friend Sit. Down Girl wakes up Rruff because she wants to be the first thing he sees in the morning. "Rruff is lucky I woke him when I did. In another hour the alarm clock would have gone off and scared him." Down Girl also successfully chases away the newspaper boy because newspapers are for spanking. "Once again I had saved my master from getting spanked." After Down Girl eats everything in sight, including acorns, flowers, sticks, birdseed, a whole sack of dog food, and a pie stolen from the table, she runs behind the couch. "Here's something odd. The couch had somehow gotten smaller."

Companion books: *On the Road* (Marshall Cavendish, 2005); *Bad to the Bone* (Marshall Cavendish, 2008); *Home on the Range* (Marshall Cavendish, 2010)

Oliver, Lin
Attack of the Growling Eyeballs
Illustrated by Stephen Gilpin. Simon & Schuster, 2008
After eating some of his great-grandmother's goulash, Daniel Funk shrinks to the size of the fourth toe on his foot. He learns that he is not the first member of the Funk lineage to do so. He also learns that he has an identical twin brother,

who was curled up inside Daniel's ear when they were born. Pablo, the twin brother, never did grow to normal size, and Granny has been keeping him a secret from the rest of the family. The whole family is strange. One of Daniel's grandmothers learned how to play the bamboo nose flute. "That's what I said. The bamboo nose flute." Daniel's sisters were named after birds: Lark, Robin, and Goldfinch. At one point, Daniel shrinks again and falls into the toilet. "Here's a tip: Do your pull-ups, friends. You never know when you'll shrink to the size of a toe and have to pull yourself onto a toilet rim."

Companion books: *Escape of the Mini-Mummy* (Simon & Schuster, 2008); *Revenge of the Itty-Bitty Brothers* (Simon & Schuster, 2009)

Palatini, Margie
Geek Chic: The Zoey Zone
Illustrated by the author. HarperCollins, 2008

Ten-year-old Zoey is worried that she's not cool. She wishes for a fairy godmother to help her out. One day, she wears her "great-grandpop's fedora" to school. She wears it with a turquoise bowling shirt with the name "Ray" on it and which advertises "Grabowski's Tool & Die Company." Zoey wishes she were more popular. She and her friend Venus are the last ones in the cafeteria line. Their remaining options are meatloaf and slumgullion. Venus chooses the latter: "She really lives on the edge." The only tables open are with the Bashleys (the popular girls Ashley and Brittany and their friends) or with Alex Shemtob, who "mostly exhales what he inhales." It's a good idea to wear art smocks when sitting across from him. One day, people from the magazine *U GrL* are at the school taking photographs. They get such a big reaction from their readers about Zoey's outfit and her locker contents that the magazine invites the suddenly cool protagonist to write her own column.

Park, Barbara
Junie B. Jones Has a Monster under Her Bed
Illustrated by Denise Brunkus. Random House, 1997

When the school photographer arrives, he gets "fusstration in him" when Junie B. doesn't cooperate. He winds up taking her picture while she's demonstrating a funny face. Her friend Lucille comments, "the camera is my friend." Paulie Allen Puffer tries to convince Junie B. that a monster lives under her bed and that the drool on her pillow is "monster drool." She runs home and hollers for her grandma Helen Miller: "I AM SO GLAD TO BE HOME! 'CAUSE TODAY WAS NOT A VERY GOOD DAY AT MY SCHOOL!" Junie adds, "'I need a hug down here, Helen.' . . . She said don't call her Helen." Later, scared of the monster under her bed, Junie climbs in bed with her parents, waking up her mother. "Mother carried me back to my room zippity quick . . . 'Do . . . *not* . . . get . . . out . . . of . . . bed . . . one . . . more . . . time,' she said."

This is the eighth book in the Junie B. Jones series, which includes more than two dozen books. The first title is *Junie B. Jones and the Stupid Smelly Bus* (Random House, 1992).

Junie B. Jones Has a Monster under Her Bed by Barbara Park

Park, Barbara
Skinnybones
Random House, 1982

Alex has a big mouth, which lands him in all kinds of trouble. He makes a mess by dumping cat food all over the kitchen floor. His mother catches him in a lie when he claims the cat knocked over the cat food and made the mess while she was gone. She gives him a look and then tells him to get the cat out of the car (she had taken it to the vet). "If you were Pinocchio . . . we could saw off your nose and have enough firewood to last the winter." The cat eats a lot of the food and throws up on Alex's shoe. His mother bursts out laughing. "For a mother, she can act extremely immature at times." Later in the story, during a baseball game, Alex reaches first base only because he shouts "BOOGA BOOGA" at the first baseman.

Companion book: *Almost Starring Skinnybones* (Random House, 1988)

Paulsen, Gary
Harris and Me
Harcourt, 1993
The language in this book is rough, but the laughs are plenty. The eleven-year-old narrator spends the summer on the northern Minnesota farm of his uncle and aunt. He spends nearly every waking minute with his nine-year-old cousin Harris. "He was wearing a set of patched bib overalls. No shirt, no shoes—just freckles and the bibs, which were so large he seemed to move inside them." Harris pulls no punches. "We heard your folks was puke drunks, is that right?" He also tells his older sister, "You can just blow it out your butt, you old cow." Immediately after breakfast one morning, the narrator chokes on a rolled-up cigarette and gets kicked by a cow. Shortly after that, the boys play war with the pigs, and Harris gets attacked by Ernie the rooster and kicked by Bill the horse.

Paulsen, Gary
How Angel Peterson Got His Name and Other Outrageous Tales about Extreme Sports
Wendy Lamb, 2003
It is author Gary Paulsen's contention that his generation participated in all sorts of extreme sports during childhood long before they became the national crazes they are today. For example, bungee jumping has been around a long time. "To understand what might have been the first bungee jump you have to understand my cousin Harris." Paulsen tells about the time Harris, whom we met in *Harris and Me* (Harcourt, 1993), jumped out of the hayloft door in a homemade bungee-jumping-like contraption and snapped back up in the air straight into a wasps' nest. "'Cut the rope! Cut the rope!' he screamed, but I had no knife and had to untie the end he had tied to the barn and my ability to untie the rope was greatly handicapped by the fact that I was laughing hysterically." At the end of the adventure, Harris says, "I wouldn't do that again even *without* the wasps."

Paulsen, Gary
Mudshark
Wendy Lamb, 2009
Twelve-year-old Lyle Williams, aka Mudshark, is the person everyone in school comes to for answers. He even helps the school principal solve the problem of the missing erasers. Each chapter opens with a humorous announcement from the principal. "Would the custodian please report to the faculty restroom with a Geiger counter, lead-lined gloves and smoked-lens goggles?" Mudshark

earned his nickname during a game of Death Ball, a combination of football, wrestling, rugby, and mudfighting. Lyle was knocked flat on his back, seemingly "down for the count." When an opposing player ran by Lyle, "one of Lyle's hands snaked out and caught the runner by an ankle. 'So fast, it was like a mudshark . . . Mudsharks lie in the mud and when something comes by, they grab it so fast that even high-speed cameras can't catch it.'"

Peck, Richard
A Long Way from Chicago
Dial, 1998

Meet Grandma Dowdel, one of the most outrageous senior citizen characters in all of children's literature. She is always fighting for the underdog by doing things like facing up to a gang of bullies or besting a crooked sheriff. Her grandchildren spend summers with her in this series of short stories set in Depression-era rural Illinois. The highlight may be the opening episode, titled "Shotgun Cheatham's Last Night above Ground," in which Grandma Dowdel succeeds in scaring a city newspaper reporter and bringing honor to one of the locals. The reporter thinks someone is rising from the dead (it was just a cat moving around the coffin), and Grandma Dowdel blasts the coffin lid with a twelve-gauge Winchester. "It was a story that grew in the telling in one of those little towns where there's always time to ponder all the different kinds of truth."

Companion books: *A Year Down Yonder* (Dial, 2000); *A Season of Gifts* (Dial, 2009)

Peck, Richard
The Teacher's Funeral: A Comedy in Three Parts
Dial, 2004

Mean, old one-room schoolhouse teacher Myrt Arbuckle dies in August, and fifteen-year-old Russell is excited. He talks about how she was past her prime and hard of hearing. "It was like a miracle, though she must have been forty." Before the funeral, Russell is dismayed to learn he has to "wear shoes and clean underdrawers to the funeral. Shoes on a weekday. Underdrawers in August. We fumed." He's also astonished that his seventeen-year-old sister, Tansy, is planning on taking a bath for the funeral. "A bath? . . . It's *Thursday*." During the funeral, Preacher Parr recalls when Myrt Arbuckle arrived in town several years before. "I don't know if you can say she was in the full bloom of her youth. I'm not sure the bloom was ever on Miss Myrt . . . she was a great big robust woman. Why, it would have taken a wagon scale to weigh her and two trips to the grain elevator to get her there." Afterward, Russell is stunned when his sister is named the new teacher.

Peck, Robert Newton
Soup
Knopf, 1974

Soup and Rob, best friends growing up in Vermont during the 1920s, are constantly pulling stunts and getting up to all sorts of antics. They deal with bullies, roll down a hill inside a barrel, and sometimes fight each other. In the episode titled "Apples and Mrs. Stetson," the boys get in trouble for flinging an apple through the church's stained-glass window. Old Mrs. Stetson runs after them, and when Rob tries to convince her that he couldn't possibly fling an apple as far as the church, she flings an apple herself to prove that it can be done. She winds up breaking old Mr. Haskin's shack window and running from trouble along with the boys.

There are more than a dozen books in this series as well as four in the Little Soup series. The second book in this series is *Soup and Me* (Knopf, 1975).

Peirce, Lincoln
Big Nate: In a Class by Himself
Illustrated by the author. HarperCollins, 2010

Nate is not exactly the most successful student. He does not have a good relationship with his teachers. "One of my all-time best nicknames for Mrs. Godfrey is Venus de Silo . . . Venus is also the name of a planet. Mrs. Godfrey is a lot like a planet. She's huge, round, and gassy." He is excited when he receives a fortune cookie that contains the following fortune: "Today you will surpass all others." As he and his friends try to figure out what he will excel at, Nate starts racking up one detention slip after another. When he finally reports to after-school detention, Mrs. Czerwicki informs him, "You appear to have established a new record . . . nobody has ever received seven detention slips in one day. Until now." Nate breaks out in a little "Woo! Woo!" dance.

Companion books: *Big Nate Strikes Again* (HarperCollins, 2010); *Big Nate on a Roll* (HarperCollins, 2011); *Big Nate: Boredom Buster* (HarperCollins, 2011). There are also compilations of the Big Nate comic series.

Pennypacker, Sara
Stuart's Cape
Illustrated by Martin Matje. Orchard, 2002

Stuart wants an adventure. He decides that he needs to have a cape in order to have an adventure. He makes a cape by stapling together one hundred old ties. Stuart proceeds to have many adventures, both imaginary and with his real-life family. In one adventure, a dinosaur, a horse, and a gorilla show up. They learn how to pretend to be Stuart. In another adventure, Stuart learns how to fly. In the chapter titled "Stuart Grows Toast," Stuart makes a list: "Why I Like Toast." His reasons include "Warm," "You can put stuff on it," and "Fits in your pocket." Stuart finds three toast seeds in his cape. "That's the kind of cape it was." He plants the seeds and "three nice, big plants popped out at once.

Like toast from a toaster, thought Stuart." The third piece of toast is enormous. Stuart and his aunt Bubbles drag it inside and cut it into pieces the size of fence posts. They share it with the neighbors. Stuart crosses "Fits in your pocket" from his list. The chapter ends with Stuart's father asking him if he's warm enough. "'Oh sure,' said Stuart. 'Warm as toast.'"

Companion book: *Stuart Goes to School* (Scholastic, 2003)

Pennypacker, Sara
The Talented Clementine

Illustrated by Marla Frazee. Hyperion, 2007

Clementine is worried when all of the third graders are assigned to perform in a fund-raising talent show called "Talent-Palooza, Night of the Stars!" The kids in her class describe their talents. Maria's act is "Cartwheel Extravaganza," and she demonstrates, crashing into the chalkboard. Another kid's act is called "Cartwheel Wham-o-Rama"—he crashes into the hamster cage. "'Now,' my teacher was saying, 'does anyone have an act that *isn't* cartwheeling?' Half the kids put their hands down." Poor Clementine doesn't have a talent to share. She takes quick tap-dancing lessons from a girl named Margaret. When Margaret's tap shoes don't fit, Clementine takes the caps of twenty-four bottles of beer off with pliers and superglues them to the bottom of her sneakers.

Companion books: *Clementine* (Hyperion, 2006); *Clementine's Letter* (Hyperion, 2008); *Clementine, Friend of the Week* (Hyperion, 2010); *Clementine and the Family Meeting* (Hyperion, 2011)

Pratchett, Terry
The Amazing Maurice and His Educated Rodents

HarperCollins, 2001

A cat named Maurice and several rats are able to talk after the rats eat some refuse from a Wizard's University dump and Maurice eats one of the rats. They join up with a pipe-playing boy named Keith in this retelling of "The Pied Piper." Trouble erupts when they enter the town of Bad Blintz and try to run their rat-catching scheme. As they're traveling to town on a mail coach, they are stopped by a highwayman. "Are there any *wizards* in there?" the robber asks. He goes on to inquire about witches, "heavily armed trolls employed by the mail coach company," werewolves, and vampires. Assured that the coach is free of all these nuisances, the highwayman brandishes his crossbow and says, "Your money *and* your life. It's a two-for-one deal, see?" He hears a noise and freezes. He is covered by rats. And he's mystified to find himself talking to a cat, who says, "Ah, there you are . . . Went straight up your trouser legs, did they?" The cat, the boy, and the rats wind up robbing the robber.

Pratchett, Terry
The Wee Free Men: A Story of Discworld
HarperCollins, 2003
Tiffany is a young witch who chases the Elf Queen for kidnapping Tiffany's little brother. Helping Tiffany are the Wee Free Men, six-inch "pictsies" with funny, heavy Scottish brogues. In one hilarious scene, the pictsie named No'-as-big-as-Medium-Sized-Jock-but-bigger-than-Wee-Jock-Jock is trying to tell Tiffany the correct way to say his name, and to impart the fact that the pictsies will be protecting her. In another scene, Tiffany is complaining about some fairy-tale characters, such as the "girl who can't tell the difference between a wolf and her grandmother." Tiffany first meets the pictsies when she notices a sheep being stolen and then catches two strange little men underneath a chicken stealing the eggs. The little men try to explain that they thought the eggs were stones and were removing these uncomfortable things from the "puir fowl."

Companion books: *A Hat Full of Sky* (HarperCollins, 2004); *Wintersmith* (HarperCollins, 2006); *I Shall Wear Midnight* (HarperCollins, 2010)

Pullman, Philip
I Was a Rat!
Illustrated by Kevin Hawkes. Knopf, 2000
One of Cinderella's rats is transformed into a boy and stays that way. We meet him as he knocks on the door of a cobbler's house, repeating over and over, "I was a rat." The laughs come when he lapses into his old rat habits, such as chewing on a pencil or a not-so-nice-lady's hand. Editions of the local newspaper, *The Daily Scourge*, are scattered throughout the book, adding to the humor. "Yes —it's official! Hunky Prince Richard has found a bride at last!" The article goes on to say "it was like something out of a fairy tale" and "By midnight, they were head over heels in love, and it only took another day for the engagement to be made official."

Rallison, Janette
My Fair Godmother
Walker, 2009
Savannah is stung when her boyfriend dumps her for her older sister. Savannah's *fair* godmother (she's not that good at her job), Chrissy, shows up. Chrissy is more concerned with shopping than granting wishes, and she sends Savannah to the Middle Ages, first as Cinderella and then as Snow White. Savannah goes back a third time to rescue Tristan, a boy in her class who was sent by Chrissy to become a prince. At one point in the book, when Savannah is Snow White, she tries hard to learn the names of the seven dwarfs. "I tried to guess his name. 'Happy?' 'Of course we are,' he said . . . Still, I tried one more time. 'No one here is Bashful?' 'Oh, I was plenty bashful when you walked in

on me while I was taking a bath.'" Savannah/Snow White eventually learns that the true names of the dwarfs are Reginald, Percival, Cedric, Edgar, Cuthbert, Ethelred, and Edwin.

Companion book: *My Unfair Godmother* (Walker, 2011)

Rex, Adam
The True Meaning of Smekday

Illustrated by the author. Hyperion, 2007

The Boov alien race has taken over Earth. They celebrate the date of their invasion (Christmas day) by renaming it Smekday. Eleven-year-old Gratuity's mother is abducted by the aliens. "When people ask me about her, I say she's very pretty. When they ask if she's smart like me, I say she's very pretty." Gratuity comments that the greeting card companies need to make a "Sorry all your friends deserted you after your alien abduction" card. When all the humans in America are ordered to resettle in Florida, Gratuity decides to drive rather than take a rocket pod. She finds her cat at the last minute (a small detail that has big implications at the end) and hits the road. Along the way, she meets a Boov named J.Lo, who has made a terrible mistake by drawing the attention of an alien race much fiercer than the Boov.

Riddell, Chris
Ottoline and the Yellow Cat

Illustrated by the author. HarperCollins, 2007

While her parents are on one of their frequent trips, Ottoline lives in a lavish apartment with Mr. Munroe, who resembles Cousin Itt from *The Addams Family*. Mr. Munroe shows Ottoline the posters he has found around town. Several lapdogs, with names like Wilson Happy-Ears McMurtagh and Fifi Fiesta Funny-Face III, are missing. Ottoline notices clues in the newspaper. Next to several articles about stolen jewelry (the victims all give funny quotes about not being able to talk about the matter) is an advertisement for a lapdog agency. Ottoline and Mr. Munroe disguise themselves and find something suspicious. And no, it's not the sock-stealing bear hiding out in the laundry room. The two unravel a lost-dog/jewelry heist operation led by a cat and a cockatoo.

Companion book: *Ottoline Goes to School* (HarperCollins, 2009)

Robinson, Barbara
The Best Christmas Pageant Ever

Illustrated by Judith Gwyn Brown. Harper & Row, 1972

The opening line will hook everyone: "The Herdmans were absolutely the worst kids in the history of the world." Teachers never held them back in a grade. "The Herdmans moved from grade to grade through the Woodrow Wilson School like those South American fish that strip your bones clean in three minutes flat . . . which was just about what they did to one teacher after another." These young troublemakers take over the lead roles of the church's annual Christmas pageant. In between stealing money from the collection plates and smoking cigars in the ladies' room, the Herdmans teach the young narrator and other members of the congregation the true meaning of "the wonder of Christmas, and the mystery of Jesus' birth."

Companion books: *The Best School Year Ever* (HarperCollins, 1994); *The Best Halloween Ever* (Joanna Cotler, 2004)

Rockwell, Thomas
How to Eat Fried Worms
Illustrated by Emily McCully. Watts, 1973

Alan bets Billy fifty dollars that he can't eat fifteen worms. They set up a list of rules: one worm a day "and he can eat them any way he wants . . . boiled, stewed, fried, fricasseed." Billy "can use ketchup or mustard or anything like that." Alan and their friend Joe provide the worms. The first worm comes from a manure pile. Billy warms up with push-ups. Alan and another friend, Tom, bring the worm in on a silver platter. "'Luddies and gintlemin!' shouted Alan. 'I prezint my musterpiece: Vurm a la Mud! . . . Would monshure like eet carved lingthvise or crussvise?'" Billy gets the worm down and realizes that it's not that bad. Alan and Joe start to worry. Later on, they are caught cheating. "Glue! You glued two crawlers together! Geez! You bunch of lousy cheats!"

Sachar, Louis
Sideways Stories from Wayside School
Illustrated by Dennis Hockerman. Follett, 1978

Wayside School was accidentally constructed "thirty stories high with one classroom per story. The builder said he was sorry." Mrs. Jewls takes over teaching the children in the classroom on the thirtieth story, with strange results. For example, Mrs. Jewls asks Dameon to run down all thirty flights to ask Louis, the yard teacher, if he would like to watch a movie with the class. Dameon runs down all thirty flights. Louis asks, "What movie?" Dameon runs all the way back up for the answer. Mrs. Jewls tells him and Dameon runs back down. "Turtles," he tells Louis. Louis asks him, "What is the movie about?" Dameon runs back up and Mrs. Jewls tells him that the movie is about turtles. Dameon runs back down and tells Louis, who says, "No thanks. I don't like turtles."

Companion books: *Wayside School Is Falling Down* (Lothrop, Lee & Shepard, 1989); *Wayside School Gets a Little Stranger* (Morrow, 1995)

Scieszka, Jon, ed.
Guys Write for Guys Read
Viking, 2005

A host of male children's and young adult authors contributed two- and three-page stories, poems, comic strips, and commentaries about being a boy to this collection. Neil Gaiman tells about how he learned that books are dangerous,

Andy Griffiths brags that his dad is better than yours, and one fact about Anthony Horowitz is that he "had a dog called Lucky but accidentally ran it over, so he changed the dog's name to Unlucky." My favorite piece is editor Jon Scieszka's contribution, titled "Brothers." He is from a family of six boys. On a family car trip, they stop at a Stuckey's restaurant and buy a pecan log roll. Once they are back on the road, their cat eats it and makes that "awful *ack ack ack* sound of a cat getting ready to barf." The cat does indeed barf, creating a chain reaction of puking boys, who "spilled out of the puke wagon and fell in the grass, gagging and yelling and laughing until we couldn't laugh anymore." Scieszka repeats this story in his autobiography, *Knucklehead: Tall Tales and Mostly True Stories about Growing Up Scieszka* (Viking, 2008).

Companion book: *Guys Read: Funny Business* (Walden Pond Press, 2010)

Scieszka, Jon
Knights of the Kitchen Table
Illustrated by Lane Smith. Viking, 1991

Joe gets a strange book as a present from his magician uncle, Joe. Along with his friends Sam and Fred, Joe gets transported by this magical book back to the time of King Arthur. The boys' adventures include battling a dragon and a very smelly giant. They find themselves facing the very angry Black Knight. The methods the quick-thinking boys use to save themselves are hilarious and include taunting the Black Knight with phrases such as "Nyah, nyah, you missed us. Nyah nyah, na nyah nyah" and "Your mother was a sardine can." When the knight charges one final time, Fred whacks the knight with a stick. "Booonnnggg!!! The helmet rang like a thousand church bells. The Black Knight sat up straight, wobbled, and then fell to the ground with an armored crash."

There are more than a dozen books in the Time Warp Trio series, as well as several television show spin-off books. The second book in the series is *The Not-So-Jolly Roger* (Viking, 1991).

Seegert, Scott
How to Grow Up and Rule the World
Illustrated by John Martin. Egmont, 2010

Vordak the Incomprehensible shares his instruction manual on how to become a supervillain. Advice is given on perfecting the evil laugh ("MUAHA-HAHAHA!"), creating a supervillain costume ("black is the color of hopelessness, of oppression . . . It is also quite slimming."), and devising nefarious schemes ("If you live in a state with bottle and can deposits, you receive 5 cents for every one you return. Do the math—20 million cans = *1 million dollars!* MUAHAHAHAHA!!!"). There is a Supervillain Power Chart, which contains the names of villains, their assumed power, and what Vordak the Incompre-

Knights of the Kitchen Table by Jon Scieszka

hensible has learned was the *actual* reason for their name. For example, it was assumed that Professor Octopus was "equipped with multiple powerful mechanical arms." Actually, he "squirts ink from bellybutton when frightened."

Snicket, Lemony
The Bad Beginning
Illustrated by Brett Helquist. HarperCollins, 1999

The first page of chapter 1 sets the tone of dark humor for the book and the series. The book has no happy beginning, middle, or end. "I'm sorry to tell you this, but that is how the story goes." The Baudelaire orphans—Violet, Klaus, and Sunny—match wits with the evil Count Olaf. The mock-Gothic atmosphere of the book is the perfect setting for the narrator's wordplay—"Occasionally his eyes would close. He found himself reading the same sentence over and over. He found himself reading the same sentence over and over. He found himself reading the same sentence over and over"—as well as the translations of baby Sunny—"For instance, this morning she was saying 'Gack!' over and over, which probably meant, 'Look at that mysterious figure emerging from the fog!'" *The Bad Beginning* features an elaborate plan by Count Olaf to marry Violet and take control of the Baudelaire family fortune.

There are thirteen books in the series. The second title is *The Reptile Room* (HarperCollins, 1999).

Spinelli, Jerry
Who Put That Hair in My Toothbrush?
Little, Brown, 1984

Two siblings—Megamouth Megin and Grosso Greg—constantly argue. They give their opposing sides of the story by narrating alternate chapters. In one episode, Greg pays their younger brother Toddie to turn on the hot water in the sink while Megin is in the shower. When her shower turns freezing cold, Megin sticks her head out and sees someone has left the bathroom door open. She tries to reach it, but has to dash for it. Just then, Toddie shows up and Megin dashes back, wrapping herself up in the shower curtain. "The curtain, like a machine gun, came pop-pop-popping off the rod; I screamed again—'YYYAAAAAAAAAAAAAAAAAAAAAAAAAHHH!'" To get back at her older brother, Megin catches a cockroach in a paper cup and uses a postcard to trap it. She carries the cup to her brother's room and crouches down in front of the closed door. "I tilted the postcard, lifted the cup. The roach ran under the door."

Spratt, R. A.
The Adventures of Nanny Piggins
Illustrated by Dan Santat. Little, Brown, 2010

Nanny Piggins is a chocolate-loving pig whose only job experience is as a flying pig in the circus (she was shot out of a cannon). She is hired by Mr.

Green to watch his three children—Derrick, Samantha, and Michael—mostly because he is a cheap man and Nanny Piggins only charges ten cents an hour. The children, of course, love her, and they all work hard to make sure she is not replaced by a regular human nanny. One night, Nanny Piggins and the children play the game of Murder in the Dark all night long. The reason the game goes on so long is that they "had simply forgotten to elect a murderer before they started." Nanny Piggins catches a young burglar who has been watching the house for some time, hoping to steal cash or jewelry. Instead of turning the juvenile delinquent over to the authorities, Nanny Piggins comes up with many inventive forms of punishment, including baking "a double-chocolate-chip chocolate mud cake with chocolate icing and chocolate sauce in the middle." She also makes the young thief cut down a tree, catch cockroaches, learn to dance the tango, and conjugate verbs. He eventually learns his lesson.

Stadler, Alexander
Julian Rodriguez: Episode One: Trash Crisis on Earth
Illustrated by the author. Scholastic, 2008
Julian Rodriguez frequently corresponds with the "Mothership." He complains about his Parental Units. They disrupt his sleep state and feed him "intergalactic space sludge," aka oatmeal. He finds it challenging to hide his intellectual superiority from "the mini-brains" at school (he attends the Aretha Franklin Elementary School). The worst thing is that Evilomami, his Maternal Unit, humiliates Julian by insisting he dispose of a "large canister, filled to the brim with humanoid refuse." The Mothership decides to beam Julian aboard and annihilate the planet. Julian stops them, stating, "The Earthlings' brains are limited . . . They know not what they do!" He decides to continue living with them. At the end of the book, Julian tells his mother, "You don't know how close you came to total annihilation today," to which his mother replies, "I was just about to say the same thing to you."
Companion book: *Episode Two: Invasion of the Relatives* (Scholastic, 2009)

Trine, Greg
Melvin Beederman, Superhero:
The Curse of the Bologna Sandwich
Illustrated by Rhode Montijo. Holt, 2006
Even though he is unable to leap a tall building in a single bound ("it always took him five or six tries"), Melvin Beederman graduates at the top of his class at the Superhero Academy. He is sent to Los Angeles ("They haven't had a superhero there since Kareem Abdul-Jabbar retired."). Every superhero has a weakness. "Melvin had found his weakness. Bologna." Later, we're introduced to the villains. "Mr. McNasty smelled bad. Mrs. McNasty smelled bad. Even their goldfish smelled bad. If you ever see extra bubbles in their fish tank, you'd better run and not look back." The McNasty brothers overcome Melvin and his sidekick, Candace, with a bologna sandwich. The chapter ends with Melvin

thinking, "'Can't . . . move . . . get . . . me . . . out . . . of . . . here.' He needed a plan." At the end of the book, the author optimistically adds that Melvin needed to "rest up for book number two."

Companion books: *Revenge of the McNasty Brothers* (Holt, 2006); *The Grateful Fred* (Holt, 2006); *Terror in Tights* (Holt, 2007); *The Fake Cape Caper* (Holt, 2007); *Attack of the Valley Girls* (Holt, 2008); *The Brotherhood of the Traveling Underpants* (Holt, 2009); *Invasion from Planet Dork* (Holt, 2010)

Voake, Steve
Daisy Dawson Is on Her Way!
Illustrated by Jessica Meserve. Candlewick, 2008

Daisy Dawson dawdles on her way to school every day and is constantly late. One day, she stops to help a butterfly out of a spider's web. As it flies away, the butterfly brushes Daisy's cheek. "Her cheek began to tingle as though something was sparkling beneath her skin." Daisy learns that she can now understand animals and speak to them. She meets Boom, a dog, who loves Daisy's ham sandwiches. Daisy also converses with two pet gerbils, a lost ant, a snobbish cat named Trixie McDixie, a horse named Meadowsweet, and Cyril the squirrel. In the episode where she meets the ant, Daisy hears a tiny voice singing, "Dubbedy dum-dum, dee dubbedy, dubbedy dum-dum, dee dubbedy." It's the ant. The ant panics when he sees Daisy. "Don't step on me with those big shoes!" Daisy convinces him that she's friendly. She correctly guesses the name of his song—"Dubbedy Dum-Dum." The ant has lost his patrol and wants to return home. Daisy helps him but is stopped by her principal on her way out. She tells the ant to shut up and the principal assumes she's talking to him.

Companion books: *Daisy Dawson and the Secret Pond* (Candlewick, 2009); *Daisy Dawson and the Big Freeze* (Candlewick, 2010); *Daisy Dawson at the Beach* (Candlewick, 2011)

Wynne-Jones, Tim
Ned Mouse Breaks Away
Illustrated by Dušan Petričić. Groundwood, 2003

Ned Mouse is sent to jail for complaining about the government. "He wrote in his pureed squash or in his custard, 'The government is unfair to mice!' And the government didn't like it one bit." Ned spends most of the book devising clever ways to escape prison, yet each attempt backfires. He is often thwarted at the last minute by a dim-witted keeper. Ned builds an airplane and tells the keeper that it's a washing machine. He takes the "washing machine" out to the yard, just in case a prisoner gets dirty. The keeper buys it. When Ned crashes the plane, the keeper tells Ned, "Maybe you didn't have enough spin on the rinse cycle." Another time, Ned tries to escape prison by hiding in a vacuum cleaner and then posing as the jail's washerwoman. When the keeper catches him, Ned tells him he has the mental capacity of a gum tree. The keeper smiles and replies that he likes gum.

Yee, Lisa
Millicent Min, Girl Genius
Scholastic, 2003

Millicent is an eleven-year-old who has skipped several grades. She makes anagrams out of her Alpha-Bits, "but the vowels keep sinking." She considers herself normal but concedes, "The complex inner workings of my brain probably scare people and repel any potential friends." She's horrified when her grandmother Maddie accompanies her to her first-period class. Hearing a disparaging remark, Maddie warns the high school students that she knows kung fu. After Maddie makes several impressive but threatening moves, the kids back away. "When she was done . . . Maddie was still in her age-defying leg-split position. 'Get up,' I hissed. 'Everyone's staring.' 'No can do,' she whispered. 'I appear to be stuck.'" When Millicent meets Emily, she decides to hide her IQ to avoid scaring her away. They become friends, but Millicent's secret inevitably comes out.

The Silliest Poetry Books

4

Agee, Jon
Orangutan Tongs: Poems to Tangle Your Tongue
Illustrated by the author. Hyperion, 2009

One highlight from this collection of tongue-twister poems is "Walter and the Waiter." Walter first complains his water is watered down, and then that it's too dry. "I like my water wet." The waiter dumps a pitcher of water over Walter's head. The poem "Dodos" relates how dodo birds do little besides dawdle, diddle, "doodle a doodle or two," yodel, and coo.

Aylesworth, Jim
The Burger and the Hot Dog
Illustrated by Stephen Gammell. Atheneum, 2001

Puns and wordplay about food are featured in this collection. In "Bums," a group of cookies is chasing a bagel. They trip and "now they're cookie crumbs." Two eggs in "Yack and Yimmy" tell jokes because "they're both so full of yolks." In "How Bleak," sticks of gum look up at the bottoms of stools and see the frightening remains of former companions.

Bagert, Brod
Giant Children
Illustrated by Tedd Arnold. Dial, 2002

A poem about boogers comes complete with a "WARNING TO ALL CHILDREN: This poem is totally disgusting, and should not, under any circumstances, be recited to a grown-up!" The best pair of poems are "Pretty Ribbon," about a brother who wants to use a snake he's found as a ribbon in his sister's hair, and "Jaws," in which the sister retaliates by encouraging a turtle to bite her brother a second time.

Brown, Calef
Soup for Breakfast: Poems and Pictures
Illustrated by the author. Houghton Mifflin, 2008

A boy dreams of having bear paws instead of hands, young children who grow up to be architects are known as "architots," and a cat turns into a two-dimensional creature when it's hot outside, but "when the temperature drops / . . . back she pops / into the third dimension." Kids will be delightedly grossed out by Grandpa's mustache when they find out it's his overly long nose hair. Grandma doesn't care. "She can't hear. Too much ear hair."

Companion book: *Flamingos on the Roof: Poems and Paintings* (Houghton Mifflin, 2006)

Dakos, Kalli
If You're Not Here, Please Raise Your Hand: Poems about School
Illustrated by G. Brian Karas. Four Winds Press, 1990

In the title poem, the teacher is tired. She says that the spelling test is Saturday night and tells the students to paint the trees on the mural with basketballs. Everyone can eat their saxophones "while I snooze in the classroom all alone. *Yawn.*" Other poems feature a boy who says he's ready to face the guillotine for the crime of not having his homework done and a child who is resigned to staying in third grade forever.

Companion books: *Don't Read This Book Whatever You Do! More Poems about School* (Four Winds Press, 1993); *Mrs. Cole on an Onion Roll and Other School Poems* (Simon & Schuster, 1995); *The Goof Who Invented Homework and Other School Poems* (Dial, 1996); *The Bug in Teacher's Coffee and Other School Poems* (HarperCollins, 1999); *Put Your Eyes Up Here and Other School Poems* (Simon & Schuster, 2003); *A Funeral in the Bathroom and Other School Bathroom Poems* (Whitman, 2011)

DiPucchio, Kelly
Sipping Spiders through a Straw
Illustrated by Gris Grimly. Scholastic, 2008

"Take Me out to the Graveyard" is sung to the tune of "Take Me out to the Ball Game," while "For He's a Stinky Old Fellow" might become a popular party substitute for the song, "For He's a Jolly Good Fellow." The other highlight is the ghoulish takeoff of "Do Your Ears Hang Low?" titled "Do Your Guts Hang Low?" "Can you tie them in a knot? / Can you feed them to a crow?"

Florian, Douglas
Bow Wow Meow Meow
Illustrated by the author. Harcourt, 2003

The subtitle, appropriately enough, is "It's Rhyming Cats and Dogs." Several breeds of both dogs and cats, including big cats like the black panther and the

If You're Not Here, Please Raise Your Hand. Poems about School by Kalli Dakos

leopard, are featured. The funniest poems feature a Persian cat who brags about being "purrrsian," a dachshund who is a limousine for fleas, a bloodhound with "scent-sational" senses, and a pointer who always "points at Frigidaires."

Companion books: *Beast Feast: Poems and Paintings* (Harcourt, 1994); *In the Swim: Poems and Paintings* (Harcourt, 1997); *Insectlopedia: Poems and Paintings* (Harcourt, 1998); *Mammalabilia: Poems and Paintings* (Harcourt, 2000); *Lizards, Frogs, and Polliwogs: Poems and Paintings* (Harcourt, 2001); *Omnibeasts: Animal Poems and Paintings* (Harcourt, 2004); *Zoo's Who: Poems and Paintings* (Harcourt, 2005); *Dinothesaurus: Prehistoric Poems and Paintings* (Atheneum, 2009)

Florian, Douglas
Laugh-eteria
Illustrated by the author. Harcourt, 1999

This collection starts with a test poem before the title page and ends with an alien lullaby in which an alien is encouraged to lay down its many heads. In between are poems about a unicorn with its horn located on its behind, an

Laugh-eteria by Douglas Florian

"aunteater" that eats aunts instead of ants, and a hot dog with the works (truly everything on it). "The poems in this book / Are meant to be humorous. / If they are not, / Please laugh just to humor us."

Grandits, John
Technically, It's Not My Fault: Concrete Poems
Illustrated by the author. Clarion, 2004

This collection of concrete poems includes a word picture of young Robert playing a game of basketball in "The Lay-Up" and another featuring baseball titled "Robert's Four At-Bats." Robert performs a long series of skateboard tricks in "Skateboard." People yell at him about skateboarding where he shouldn't. He gives it up. His parents then complain, "You begged for that skateboard, Robert. Now go out and use it!" The highlight is Robert's "The Thank-You Letter," complete with sarcastic footnotes.

Companion book: *Blue Lipstick: Concrete Poems* (Clarion, 2007)

Hoberman, Mary Ann
You Read to Me, I'll Read to You: Very Short Fairy Tales to Read Together
Illustrated by Michael Emberley. Little, Brown, 2004

Each poem is designed for two voices. In most cases, the adversaries settle their differences and read their own stories to each other. Little Red Riding Hood lets the wolf know that she doesn't believe he is her grandmother for one minute. The biggest billy goat learns that the troll needs the money he makes from allowing creatures to cross the bridge to support his brothers. The troll is sorry he frightened the goats.

Companion books: *You Read to Me, I'll Read to You: Very Short Stories to Read Together* (Little, Brown, 2001); *You Read to Me, I'll Read to You: Very Short Mother Goose Tales to Read Together* (Little, Brown, 2005); *You Read to Me, I'll Read to You: Very Short Scary Tales to Read Together* (Little, Brown, 2007); *You Read to Me, I'll Read to You: Very Short Fables to Read Together* (Little, Brown, 2010)

Katz, Alan
Take Me out of the Bathtub and Other Silly Dilly Songs
Illustrated by David Catrow. Margaret K. McElderry, 2001

Katz has created new lyrics to popular songs. "Stinky Stinky Diaper Change" is set to the tune of "Twinkle, Twinkle, Little Star"; "Go Go Go to Bed" is to be sung to "Row, Row, Row Your Boat"; and "Give Me a Break," a complaint about overdue library books, is set to the tune of "Home on the Range."

Companion books: *I'm Still Here in the Bathtub: Brand New Silly Dilly Songs* (Margaret K. McElderry, 2003); *Where Did They Hide My Presents? Silly Dilly Christmas Songs* (Margaret K. McElderry, 2005); *Smelly Locker: Silly Dilly School Songs* (Margaret K. McElderry, 2008); *On Top of the Potty and Other Get-Up-and-Go Songs* (Margaret K. McElderry, 2008); *Too Much*

You Read to Me, I'll Read to You: Very Short Fairy Tales to Read Together by Mary Ann Hoberman

Kissing! and Other Silly Dilly Songs about Parents (Margaret K. McElderry, 2009); *Mosquitoes Are Ruining My Summer! and Other Silly Dilly Camp Songs* (Margaret K. McElderry, 2011)

Kennedy, X. J.
Exploding Gravy: Poems to Make You Laugh
Illustrated by Joy Allen. Little, Brown, 2002

The very first poem in the book, "Mother's Nerves," sets the tone. Mother threatens to jump into the stove the next time the screen door slams, and sure enough, "I gave it a bang and in she dove." Another highlight is the limerick tribute to reading, "Hooked on Books." A man continues to read a book after he hangs his coat on the hook (the man is still wearing the coat).

Lansky, Bruce, ed.
Oh My Darling, Porcupine, and Other Silly Sing-Along Songs
Illustrated by Stephen Carpenter. Meadowbrook, 2006

One of the more gross (but still silly) songs is "The Top of My Hot Dog," set to the tune of "On Top of Old Smoky," in which a seagull deposits a topping for the narrator's hot dog. Another silly poem is the lengthy "Bring Back My Sister to Me," set to the tune of "My Bonnie." Sister falls down the toilet. She's followed by brother, father, mother, kitty, and dog.

Lewis, J. Patrick
Once upon a Tomb: Gravely Humorous Verses
Illustrated by Simon Bartram. Candlewick, 2006

Lewis composed twenty-two epitaphs for an underwear salesman, dairy farmer, fisherman, poet, fortune-teller, food critic, principal, tattoo artist, movie star, bully, soccer player, beautician, weight lifter, cafeteria lady, and more. There's even one for a grave digger pointing out that it's a good thing he died or "He'd have to dig himself a hole."

Prelutsky, Jack
Awful Ogre's Awful Day
Illustrated by Paul O. Zelinsky. Greenwillow, 2001

Awful Ogre boasts that he's "awfulest of all." In "Awful Ogre Pens a Letter," he writes to an ogress that he longs for her "craggy gray face." He also calls her "Demure and petite, / Just fourteen-foot-four / From your head to your feet." The collection ends with "Awful Ogre's Awful Dream," in which Awful Ogre dreams about meandering through a beautiful landscape. "I have never had a nightmare / Nearly half this bad before."

Companion book: *Awful Ogre Running Wild* (Greenwillow, 2008)

Prelutsky, Jack
The New Kid on the Block
Illustrated by James Stevenson. Greenwillow, 1984

This is the first in a series of solid humorous poetry collections cocreated by Prelutsky and Stevenson. Highlights include the title poem, with its surprise tagline, and the poem "Dainty Dottie Dee," which features a compulsive house cleaner who even cleans the garbage before throwing it out. Other favorites to read aloud are "Be Glad Your Nose Is on Your Face," "When Tillie Ate the Chili," and "Boing! Boing! Squeak!"

Companion books: *Something Big Has Been Here* (Greenwillow, 1990); *A Pizza the Size of the Sun* (Greenwillow, 1996); *It's Raining Pigs and Noodles* (Greenwillow, 2000); *My Dog May Be a Genius* (Greenwillow, 2008)

Rex, Adam
Frankenstein Makes a Sandwich
Illustrated by the author. Harcourt, 2006

The titles of the poems give clues to the zany content of this collection devoted to movie monsters: "The Phantom of the Opera Can't Get 'It's a Small World' Out of His Head," "The Creature from the Black Lagoon Doesn't Wait an Hour before Swimming," "Bigfoot Can't Believe You Called Him Yeti Just Now," and my favorite, "Count Dracula Doesn't Know He's Been Walking around All Night with Spinach in His Teeth."

Companion book: *Frankenstein Takes the Cake* (Harcourt, 2008)

Scieszka, Jon
Science Verse
Illustrated by Lane Smith. Viking, 2004

These poems deal with different aspects of science and are written in the style of famous poems. For example, "Astronaut Stopping by a Planet on a Snowy Evening" is inspired by Robert Frost's poem "Stopping by Woods on a Snowy Evening." A highlight is the adaptation of "Jack Be Nimble." Instead of jumping over a candlestick, Jack jumps over "the combustion reaction of O_2 + heat + fuel to form CO_2 + light + heat + exhaust."

Companion book: *Math Curse* (Viking, 1995) (This book is not a poetry book, but it is very funny.)

Shields, Carol Diggory
Someone Used My Toothbrush and Other Bathroom Poems
Illustrated by Paul Meisel. Dutton, 2010

The bathroom is an important room in the house. "Soaked 1" shows what happens when you bathe a dog, and "Soaked 2" warns of the hazards of bathing a cat. A boy has trouble sleeping in "Drip." The medicine cabinet contains everything under the sun: "Sprays for noses, feet, and pits / Half-a-dozen cures for zits." The book's title poem tells of a worried boy who believes his sister used his toothbrush "to scrub our pet iguana."

Sierra, Judy
Monster Goose
Illustrated by Jack E. Davis. Harcourt, 2001
What if Mother Goose was actually an evil goose who cranked out ghoulish nursery rhymes? Little Miss Muffet becomes "Little Miss Mummy," the old woman who lived in a shoe is transformed in "There Was an Old Zombie," Little Bo Peep becomes "Werewolf Bo-Creep," and Little Jack Horner becomes "Cannibal Horner," who "Sat in a corner / Eating a people potpie."

Silverstein, Shel
Where the Sidewalk Ends
Illustrated by the author. Harper & Row, 1974
This is the touchstone collection of children's humorous poetry. Generations of schoolchildren are familiar with "Jimmy Jet and His TV Set," "Boa Constrictor," "Sick," "Sarah Cynthia Sylvia Stout Would Not Take the Garbage Out," "Peanut-Butter Sandwich," "For Sale," "The Crocodile's Toothache," "The Farmer and the Queen," and even the tenderhearted "Hug o' War" where "everyone wins."

Companion books: *A Light in the Attic* (Harper & Row, 1981); *Falling Up* (HarperCollins, 1996); *Every Thing On It* (HarperCollins, 2011)

Viorst, Judith
If I Were in Charge of the World and Other Worries
Illustrated by Lynne Cherry. Atheneum, 1981
Here it is—my all-time favorite collection of children's humorous poetry. The title poem finds the narrator wishing for "basketball baskets forty-eight inches lower" and no more sisters. Other highlights include "Learning," "Some Things Don't Make Any Sense at All," "And Then the Prince Knelt Down and Tried to Put the Glass Slipper on Cinderella's Foot," and the poem whose title is four times as long as the poem: "Thoughts on Getting Out of a Nice, Warm Bed in an Ice-Cold House to Go to the Bathroom at Three o'Clock in the Morning."

Companion book: *Sad Underwear and Other Complications* (Atheneum, 1995)

Weinstock, Robert
Can You Dig It? and Other Poems
Illustrated by the author. Hyperion, 2010
This collection of poems features dinosaurs and aspects of early human life. The highlight is "Coprolite," which tells about LuAnn Abrue, a paleontologist who was famous for "finding fossil poo / Like giant T. rex number two." LuAnn was often heard to say, "You are not only what you eat, / You also are what you excrete."

The Silliest Graphic Novels and Manga ⑤

Bliss, Harry
Luke on the Loose
Illustrated by the author. Toon Books, 2009

A little boy named Luke is in Central Park with his father when all of a sudden, he takes off after some pigeons. We follow Luke as he and the pigeons startle a dog and its owner, cross the Brooklyn Bridge, zip through a sidewalk café, and disrupt kids at an ice cream stand. One alley has a wanted poster for the Incredible Hulk. As Luke tears through the café, he interrupts a man proposing to his girlfriend. After the chaos has passed, the man asks, "But Sofi . . . When you say 'EEK! AAAH! HELP! HELP!' is that a YES?" Luke eventually crawls onto the roof of a building and is rescued by the fire department. The last picture shows Luke and his father back in the park. Luke is reaching for some pigeons, but he is now wearing a leash.

Davis, Eleanor
The Secret Science Alliance and the Copycat Crook
Illustrated by the author. Bloomsbury, 2009

Julian's an Ultra Nerd. He tries to show his new classmates that he's normal by declaring that he hangs out at the mall and enjoys watching television. His cover is blown when his teacher asks, "What can you tell me about propellers?" Julian sleepily replies, "The propeller spinning creates a pressure difference, which causes air to be accelerated through the blades. This generates thrust and pushes the vehicle forward . . . in accordance with the first law . . ." Julian comes to and notices everyone looking at him. He is surprised to learn that the school's best athlete and its most notorious girl are scientific geniuses. Together, they form the Secret Science Alliance. A notebook of their inventions is stolen

131

by Dr. Wilhelm Stringer. The alliance ultimately uses their inventions against him. These include the "Pop Open Kick Me Sign," the "Secret Squirt Watch Filled with Stink Ink," and the "Exploding Itching-Powder Pellet."

Davis, Eleanor
Stinky
Illustrated by the author. Toon Books, 2008
A small monster named Stinky is proud of his smelly swamp and cave. The small woodland animals and birds that live near Stinky's cave have clothespins on their noses and beaks. Stinky is a bit nervous about the nearby town. "Towns have kids . . . and kids don't like swamps. They like to take baths!" One kid named Nick, however, enjoys the swamp and builds a tree house in it. Stinky tries to scare Nick away by placing his overgrown toad, Wartbelly, in the tree house. Nick loves Wartbelly and calls him Daisy. Nick eventually saves Stinky from the Bottomless Pit, and the two become friends.

Elder, Joshua
Mail Order Ninja, Vol. 1
Illustrated by Erich Owen. TokyoPop, 2006
Timmy wins a contest and receives a real live ninja named Yoshido Jiro. The biographical information about Jiro states that he "once had a promising music career and was dubbed the 'Japanese Barry Manilow' by critics." Timmy's parents inform their son that "owning a ninja is a big responsibility. Remember what happened with the iguana?" Timmy objects—who knew the iguana "would just explode like that?" While Timmy is explaining to his parents that his ninja wouldn't hurt a fly, the ninja is smashing a fly in the background. "Okay, so that was a bad example, but please, Mom . . ." The ninja helps Timmy deal with school bullies and win the school election. "Timmy = 984, Felicity = 2, Seymour Butts = 3."
 Companion book: *Mail Order Ninja, Vol. 2* (TokyoPop, 2006)

Gownley, Jimmy
Amelia Rules! The Whole World's Crazy
Illustrated by the author. Atheneum, 2006
Amelia's parents are divorced. Amelia and her mother move in with her aunt Tanner. She slowly learns that her new friends—Reggie, Pajamaman, and frenemy Rhonda—are the school nerds. "Now I'm a nerd by association!" Reggie matter-of-factly explains that the "sneeze barf" is also known as "Sneezicus Barfona." The four of them play superhero games and eventually meet up with other kids who are just as imaginative.
 There are more than a dozen books featuring Amelia. The second title in the series is *Amelia Rules! What Makes You Happy* (Atheneum, 2009).

Guibert, Emmanuel
Sardine in Outer Space 4
Illustrated by Joann Sfar. First Second, 2007

Sardine has intergalactic adventures with her space pirate uncle Captain Yellow Shoulder, her cousin Little Louie, and her black cat. They frequently encounter their nasty adversaries Supermuscleman, who is the Chief Executive Dictator of the Universe, and his mad scientist henchman, Doc Krok. This volume of the series is highlighted because of the fun opening story, titled "Under the Bed." Sardine heads under the bed looking for Little Louie and instead finds the leaping sheep "who leap over your bed at night"; the sheep's sheepdog Shep, who is manning a Lost and Found station; and Nightmurray, the monster under the bed, who starts crying. Sardine transfers Nightmurray to Supermuscleman's bed and the leaping sheep to Doc Krok's bed.

There are eight books in the series. They all have the same title and a volume number.

Harper, Charise Mericle
Fashion Kitty
Illustrated by the author. Hyperion, 2005

The Kittie family, a family of cats, is unusual. First, they have a pet mouse named Mousie, aka Phoebe Frederique (the Kittie family members are all vegetarian). Second, the two girl kittens, Kiki and Lana, get to choose their own clothes ("Mother Kittie believes in free fashion"), and third, they know the secret identity of Fashion Kitty (it's Kiki, who was hit on the head by a pile of fashion magazines just as she was making a birthday wish and blowing out the candles). There's a two-page spread on "boys don't give two hoots about fashion." Various boys give their reasons: "I wear the same thing every day. But my mom makes me change my socks and my underwear"; "This is my favorite shirt. I've been wearing it for three years. It's a little short." In this, her first adventure, Fashion Kitty saves someone from committing a fashion faux pas.

Companion books: *Fashion Kitty versus the Fashion Queen* (Hyperion, 2007); *Fashion Kitty and the Unlikely Hero* (Hyperion, 2008); *Fashion Kitty and the B.O.Y.S. (Ball of Yellow String)* (Hyperion, 2011)

Holm, Jennifer L.
Babymouse: Queen of the World
Illustrated by Matthew Holm. Random House, 2005

Babymouse doesn't have many expectations. "Well, maybe a few." We see her wishing for a tiara, straight whiskers, ice cream for lunch, and no homework. Babymouse is obsessed with attending Felicia Furrypaws's slumber party. Once she gets to it, she's bored. Babymouse drops a curling iron on a rug and gets nail polish all over Felicia. She worries about her friend Wilson and realizes

Babymouse: Queen of the World by Jennifer L. Holm

that she's already a queen. "My life IS great." The narrator says that we knew she'd figure it out eventually, to which Babymouse replies, "You don't have to rub it in." In one of Babymouse's many imagination scenes, she pictures herself as Babymouserella. Her fairy godmother says, "I prefer 'Fairy Godweasel.'"

There are more than fifteen books featuring Babymouse. The second in the series is *Babymouse: Our Hero* (Random House, 2005).

Kitamura, Satoshi
Comic Adventures of Boots
Illustrated by the author. Farrar Straus Giroux, 2002

A cat named Boots stars in three stories in this graphic novel. The first story shows Boots tricking other cats so they have to move off a wall and make space for him. The second story shows a duck saving Boots from drowning. Boots learns to swim afterward and asks the duck to teach him how to fly. In the last story, "Let's Play a Guessing Game," different cats act as a penguin, a cat hanging on to a cliff, a rabbit in its burrow, an owl, and a dog ("Max at the Maxwells' to be precise"). When one cat scrunches up his face to suggest a chameleon, we see him saying, "Oh, no! I can't put my face back."

Krosoczka, Jarrett J.
Lunch Lady and the Cyborg Substitute
Illustrated by the author. Knopf, 2009

Three students—Hector, Dee, and Terrence—imagine that their lunch lady is a secret agent. It turns out that she is. Lunch Lady is suspicious of the new substitute teacher, Mr. Pasteur, because he won't eat her famous French toast sticks. She enters her secret boiler room lair behind the cafeteria refrigerator and arms herself with a "Spatu-copter," a combination spatula and helicopter. Lunch Lady also has a spork phone, chicken nugget bombs, and fish stick nunchucks to help her fight evildoers. She follows Mr. Pasteur on her scooter. "I'm on him like cheese on macaroni." She learns that he's a robot working for another teacher, Mr. Edison, in his quest to be the Teacher of the Year! The story ends with Lunch Lady trying out her new Electronic Bananarang.

Companion books: *Lunch Lady and the League of Librarians* (Knopf, 2009); *Lunch Lady and the Author Visit Vendetta* (Knopf, 2009); *Lunch Lady and the Summer Camp Shakedown* (Knopf, 2010); *Lunch Lady and the Bake Sale Bandit* (Knopf, 2010); *Lunch Lady and the Field Trip Fiasco* (Knopf, 2011); *Lunch Lady and the Mutant Mathletes* (Knopf, 2012)

Lechner, John
Sticky Burr: Adventures in Burrwood Forest
Illustrated by the author. Candlewick, 2007

Sticky Burr is a unique burr. He'd rather paint and play his ukulele than "do prickly things" like the other burrs. Scurvy Burr, a bully, tries to get Sticky

Burr kicked out of the village. Sticky Burr saves the village from a pack of wild dogs. He leads the dogs away with the help of lightning bugs. Scurvy Burr is resentful of Sticky Burr's heroics. He complains, "What are you going to do now—give him a parade?" The other burrs think that's a great idea. "And a party too!" When Scurvy Burr says that they haven't heard the last of him, another burr says, "Why, are you going to sing a song?" In a little aside for the adults, Sticky's friend Mossy Burr takes karate lessons from a grasshopper. She tells her instructor, "Thank you, Grasshopper," a reference to the old *Kung Fu* television series.

Companion book: *Sticky Burr: The Prickly Peril* (Candlewick, 2009)

Morse, Scott
Magic Pickle
Illustrated by the author. Graphix/Scholastic, 2008

Jo Jo wakes up when a superpowered pickle bursts through her bedroom floor. The pickle is called Weapon Kosher and was created fifty years earlier by Doctor Formaldehyde. Both Jo Jo and Weapon Kosher battle evil superpowered vegetables known as the Brotherhood of Evil Produce. When Jo Jo first encounters Weapon Kosher, she's wearing "footsie jammies." After their first battle with the Brotherhood, the magic pickle drops Jo Jo off at her school bus stop. She hides from the other kids. "I will not be seen in public in footsie jammies." The climax takes place in the school cafeteria when Jo Jo starts a food fight. The duo is able to stop the evil Romaine Gladiator by throwing him in a garbage disposal.

Companion books: *Magic Pickle and the Planet of the Grapes* (Graphix/Scholastic, 2008); *Magic Pickle versus the Egg Poacher* (Graphix/Scholastic, 2008); *Magic Pickle and the Garden of Evil* (Graphix/Scholastic, 2009); *Magic Pickle and the Creature from the Black Legume* (Graphix/Scholastic, 2009)

Petrucha, Stefan
Harry Potty and the Deathly Boring
Illustrated by Rick Parker. Papercutz, 2010

Whiny Stranger, aka Hermione Granger, gives a recap of the first Harry Potter books with her magic spell "Rememberallthisstufficis!" During the recap of the first book, we learn that Valuemart has survived by appearing on the "butt of the nervous Defense Against Dark Farts Professor Squirrel." The scar on Harry's forehead keeps changing throughout the book. The events from the final Harry Potter book are played out. Throughout this parody, we find the various Harry Potter characters—Headmaster Always Dumb-as-a-Door, Don Measley, Earwig the owl, Haggard, Frappe (Snape), the Sorting Sock, and Valuemart, aka "He-Whose-Prices-Can't-Be-Beat."

The Adventures of Ook and Gluk, Kung-Fu Cavemen from the Future by Dav Pilkey

Pilkey, Dav
The Adventures of Ook and Gluk, Kung-Fu Cavemen from the Future
Illustrated by the author. Scholastic, 2010

The boys from the Captain Underpants series—George and Harold—have created their own comic book, complete with misspellings, about two kids who "lived way back in the year 500,001 B.C. in a villege called Caveland, Ohio." They battle the evil Chief Goppernopper, whose descendant comes from the future through a time portal to plunder ancient Earth of its natural resources. The "Cavemonics" lessons at the end of the book teach readers how to talk like cavemen. For example, "My grandmother doesn't think this book belongs in the school library" turns into "Grandma no fun" in caveman talk.

Pilkey, Dav
The Adventures of Super Diaper Baby
Illustrated by the author. Scholastic, 2002

This offering by Pilkey's characters George and Harold gives the origin of Super Diaper Baby. The doctor who delivers him gives him a hearty slap ("It's a tradishon. All docters do this.")—and the baby flies out a window and lands in a container of superpower juice held by Deputy Dangerous. Super Diaper Baby's parents decide to name him Billy. At one point, as Super Diaper Baby flies off to battle the Robo-Ant 2000, his mother yells out, "Billy, don't be a hero." Later on, Super Diaper Baby and Diaper Dog fly to the planet Uranus. A sign reads, "Welcome to Uranus. Please don't make fun of our name."

Companion book: *Super Diaper Baby 2: The Invasion of the Potty Snatchers* (Scholastic, 2011)

Proimos, James
The Many Adventures of Johnny Mutton
Illustrated by the author. Harcourt, 2001

A baby sheep is left on Momma Mutton's doorstep, and "Momma's weak eyes and warm heart kept her from even noticing" that he's a sheep. She raises him as a human child. Johnny stands out by bringing marshmallows to his teacher instead of an apple. For Halloween, he dresses as a runny nose. The other kids make fun of him, except for Gloria Crust, who is dressed as a giant box of tissues. At one point, Johnny calls his mother mean because she spends time on her tuba lessons instead of helping him practice for a spelling bee. However, when asked to spell "love," Johnny responds, "M-O-M-M-A."

Companion books: *Johnny Mutton, He's So Him!* (Harcourt, 2003); *Mutton Soup: More Adventures of Johnny Mutton* (Harcourt, 2004)

Reynolds, Aaron
Joey Fly, Private Eye, in Creepy Crawly Crime
Illustrated by Neil Numberman. Holt, 2009

This noir graphic novel features a sleuth who has been asked to find a butterfly's missing diamond pencil box. "Life in the bug city. It ain't easy. Crime sticks to this city like a one-winged fly on a fifty-cent swatter." With his brand-new assistant, the young scorpion Sammy Stingtail, the fly detective questions a ladybug named Gloria and a mosquito named Flittany. Flittany calls Joey Fly a pinhead. Joey's narrative voice-over says, "She had been trying to insult me, but the laugh was on her. My head really is the size of a pin."

Companion book: *Joey Fly, Private Eye, in Big Hairy Drama* (Holt, 2010)

Sonishi, Kenji
Leave It to PET! The Misadventures of a Recycled Super Robot
Illustrated by the author. Vizkids, 2004

PET is a tiny super robot created from a plastic bottle that was recycled by nine-year-old Noboru. PET promises to help Noboru in any way to show his gratitude for being recycled. The trouble is that PET never comes through on his assignments. Noboru captures a grasshopper and wants PET to hold it for him. Unfortunately, PET pops the grasshopper into a container with a praying mantis. After the praying mantis eats the grasshopper, PET develops a "Pet-Bio-Regeneration Project!" He genetically (and miraculously) re-creates the grasshopper—and then pops him back in with the praying mantis. The praying mantis eats the grasshopper again. PET teaches Noboru the following distress call: "Pa-Pi-Pu-Pe! Pi-Pu-Pe-Po! Po-Pu-Pe-Pa PET! One tiny slip-up and it won't work!" Of course, when Noboru is threatened by bullies, he can't remember the complicated distress call sequence. "Pa-Po-Pi-Pu? Po-Pu-Pe-Po?"

There are eight volumes featuring PET. All have the same title and a volume number.

Spiegelman, Nadja
Zig and Wikki in Something Ate My Homework
Illustrated by Trade Loeffler. Toon Books, 2010

Two aliens land on Earth to complete Zig's homework assignment: get a pet for the class zoo. They try to catch a fly, but it gets away. They also encounter dragonflies, a frog, and a raccoon. Wikki dresses up like a cowboy to catch the frog. The two aliens wind up on a lily pad. Wikki says, "I tied this rope to its leg!" The moment Zig says, "You did WHAT?" the frog, who is underwater, takes off, pulling the lily pad. When the raccoon turns on them, they quickly take off. They are sad that they didn't complete their homework assignment. Then they notice the fly buzzing around inside the spaceship—it had flown in while they weren't looking. Mission accomplished.

Spires, Ashley
Binky the Space Cat
Illustrated by the author. Kids Can, 2009

Binky is a house cat who believes he needs to protect his humans from "aliens." The aliens are really bugs. Binky joins F.U.R.S.T., which stands for Felines of the Universe Ready for Space Travel. Binky trains hard, wearing a bandana and kicking a hanging "pretend alien." He builds a rocket ship but finds it painful to leave his humans. "No more Binky, Space Cat Extraordinaire." After swallowing a fly, he realizes that he has made the right choice because "his humans are utterly helpless without him." The copyright page contains the following announcement: "No aliens, bugs, or Space Cats were harmed in the making of this book. Okay, a mosquito was batted away a little too enthusiastically, and a fruit fly drowned under slightly suspicious circumstances, but that's all. Space Cat's honor."

Companion books: *Binky to the Rescue* (Kids Can, 2010); *Binky under Pressure* (Kids Can, 2011)

Steinberg, D. J.
The Adventures of Daniel Boom aka Loud Boy: Game On!
Illustrated by Brian Smith. Grosset & Dunlap, 2009

A group of kids have "pretty extraordinary abilities." They fight "an international web of cranky people known as Kid-Rid." The villain called Old Fogey has a plan to digitally insert kids into a popular computer game called Pig Planet. The final device that the villains need looks like a banana. Uncle Stanley, who is a good guy, has the banana. He asks the kids to meet him at the zoo, where he is disguised as an ape. When the bad guys appear, Uncle Stanley is in the enclosed glass cage dressed up as an ape, holding up cue cards for Daniel Boom, who is being interrogated by Old Fogey.

Companion books: *The Adventures of Daniel Boom aka Loud Boy: Sound Off!* (Grosset & Dunlap, 2008); *The Adventures of Daniel Boom aka Loud Boy: Mac Attack!* (Grosset & Dunlap, 2008); *The Adventures of Daniel Boom aka Loud Boy: Grow Up!* (Grosset & Dunlap, 2010)

Townsend, Michael
Kit Feeny: On the Move
Illustrated by the author. Knopf, 2009

Kit moves from the country to town and leaves behind his best friend, Arnold. Kit makes a comic book with Arnold. It is titled "The Great Gummy Fish Disaster: A True Story" and recounts the time Kit and Arnold poured Jell-O powder into his twin sisters' goldfish bowl and then set the whole thing in the refrigerator. Kit decides to give his classmates an "Arnold test" to see who will be his new best friend. Unfortunately, he runs into Devon the Comedian, a bully. Kit thinks of a clever way to deal with Devon and learns that, while no one will replace Arnold, he can still make new friends.

Companion book: *Kit Feeny: The Ugly Necklace* (Knopf, 2009)

Venable, Colleen
Hamster and Cheese
Illustrated by Stephanie Yue. Lerner, 2010

Sasspants the guinea pig is mistaken for a private investigator when the "g" in "pig" on the sign outside his cage falls off (leaving "Guinea PI"). He lives with several other animals at Mr. Venezi's Pets & Stuff pet store. (Mr. Venezi is slightly confused. He's labeled the snakes as llamas, the mice as walruses, the goldfish as a three-toed sloth, and the hamsters as koalas.) Sasspants is asked to solve the mystery of Mr. Venezi's stolen sandwiches. The hamster who hires

Sasspants is worried that he will be blamed. Sasspants interviews several fish as eyewitnesses to the crime. Their responses are all over the place. One claims, "I can describe the thief," while another says, "I like bread." Based on their collective comments, the sketch artist comes up with a drawing of the stolen sandwich instead of the thief.

Companion books: *And Then There Were Gnomes* (Lerner, 2010); *The Ferret's a Foot* (Lerner, 2011); *Fish You Were Here* (Lerner, 2011)

The Robbie Hall of Fame Guide to the Funniest Children's Authors and Illustrators

The Top Ten (actually 11)

BEVERLY CLEARY

Why does she make us laugh? Cleary shows the everyday challenges of growing up, with a gentle writing style in which the humor sometimes sneaks up on you and sometimes is in your face. Ramona Quimby is a funny, independent, sometimes stubborn little girl who paved the way for other characters such as Barbara Parks's Junie B. Jones, Megan McDonald's Judy Moody, and Sara Pennypacker's Clementine. I even see Ramona in some nonhuman characters such as Ian Falconer's Olivia. Cleary's humor can be found not only in the Henry Huggins series and the Ramona series showcased in this book, but also in the Ralph S. Mouse series and the Jimmy and Janet picture books.

DOREEN CRONIN

Why does she make us laugh? Like many of her fellow Top Eleven authors, she makes sure there are enough levels of humor to tickle the funny bones of her young target audience while keeping mom and dad laughing as well. She sometimes draws on her legal background to throw in contract language, as when the animal characters of *Dooby Dooby Moo* are told that there are real-life stipulations to winning a contest prize. *Diary of a Worm* and *Dooby Dooby Moo*, titles from two of her popular series, and *Rescue Bunnies* are included in this book. Other Cronin books worth checking out include *Wiggle* and *M.O.M. (Mom Operating Manual)*.

ROALD DAHL

Why does he make us laugh? Dahl's fantastic settings and unforgettable characters best demonstrate his irreverent humor as the little people, such as Matilda and James, triumph over the evil, often cloddish authority figures. *The BFG*, *Matilda*, and *The Twits* are showcased in this book. Other notable funny Dahl books include *Charlie and the Chocolate Factory*, *Fantastic Mr. Fox*, *James and the Giant Peach*, *Revolting Rhymes*, and his autobiography, *Boy: Tales of Childhood*.

ROBERT MUNSCH

Why does he make us laugh? This storyteller-author's strengths lie in the tools of oral tradition: rhythm, repetition, and audience participation. His unique characters often appear in bizarre circumstances. Perhaps best known for his tenderhearted book *Love You Forever*, his humor shines in *Alligator Baby*, *Mortimer*, *Mud Puddle*, *The Paper Bag Princess*, and *ZOOM!* His books *Moira's Birthday*, *Stephanie's Ponytail*, and *Thomas' Snowsuit* are featured in this book.

MARGIE PALATINI

Why does she make us laugh? She is the queen of puns and alliteration. She sneaks in a lot of allusions to traditional rhymes and folktales. There are many levels of humor found in her books. Sometimes the kids will laugh at one thing and the adults will laugh at another. In addition to *Piggie Pie!* and *Bad Boys*, both featured in this book, a sampling of her other funniest works includes *Earthquack!*, *Lousy Rotten Stinkin' Grapes*, *The Three Silly Billies*, and my favorite, *The Web Files* (sadly out of print).

JON SCIESZKA AND LANE SMITH

Why do they make us laugh? Whether you look at their collaborative works or their individual titles, this pair is consistent with their humor but always looking for new topics to poke fun at. They began with retellings of old folktales, turning them into *The True Story of the Three Little Pigs*, *The Frog Prince, Continued*, *The Stinky Cheese Man*, and *Squids Will Be Squids*, all featured in this book. Also represented here are a few of their non-folklore-based books (some of which are independent efforts), such as *Guys Read*, *Science Verse*, *It's a Book*, *John, Paul, George, and Ben*, and the Time Warp Trio series. Look also for Scieszka's *Robot Zot* and the Trucktown series as well as Smith's *Madam President* and the Happy Hocky Family easy readers.

DR. SEUSS

Why does he make us laugh? His humor is timeless. Many have tried to duplicate his whimsical verse and odd-sounding names, but they cannot quite capture the essence of his humor. Pretty much anything he's created will provide a good laugh. In addition to the books featured here—*The Cat in the Hat*, *Green Eggs and Ham*, *Horton Hatches the Egg*, *I Wish That I Had Duck*

Feet (as Theo LeSieg), *One Fish, Two Fish, Red Fish, Blue Fish, The Sneetches,* and *Yertle the Turtle*—check out *The 500 Hats of Bartholomew Cubbins, Hop on Pop, If I Ran the Zoo,* and *McElligot's Pool.*

SHEL SILVERSTEIN

Why does he make us laugh? His irreverent verse showcases outrageous characters and situations. Like Dr. Seuss, Silverstein has had many imitators who don't quite reach his quality of humor. The books *Where the Sidewalk Ends* and *Who Wants a Cheap Rhinoceros?* are both featured here. Check out his books *Lafcadio, the Lion Who Shot Back, The Missing Piece,* and *Runny Babbit,* in addition to his other collections of poetry.

JUDITH VIORST

Why does she make us laugh? In addition to having some of the longest children's book titles in children's literature, Viorst points out the little nagging aspects of a child's life. By broadcasting them, she makes them funny. Her picture book *Alexander and the Terrible, Horrible, No Good, Very Bad Day* and her poetry book *If I Were in Charge of the World* are both featured here. Also look up her picture books *Super-Completely and Totally the Messiest* and *My Mama Says There Aren't Any Zombies, Ghosts, Vampires, Creatures, Demons, Monsters, Fiends, Goblins, or Things.*

MO WILLEMS

Why does he make us laugh? He successfully uses his background as an animator to portray characters like Pigeon (represented in this guide) and Elephant and Piggie. He observes family dynamics and documents them in funny scenarios, as in the Knuffle Bunny books (also included here). And he's so darn prolific! Every time you turn around, there's another funny Willems book. Check out some of his other titles, such as *Edwina, the Dinosaur Who Didn't Know She Was Extinct, Leonardo the Terrible Monster,* and *Time to Pee.*

Illustration Credits

Page 2. Illustration from *Milo's Hat Trick,* by Jon Agee. Text and illustration copyright © 2001 by Jon Agee. A Michael di Capua Book, published by Hyperion Books for Children, a division of Disney Book Group. Reprinted by permission of Pippin Properties. All rights reserved.

Page 17. Text and illustrations from *Bark, George,* by Jules Feiffer. Text and illustrations copyright © 1999 by Jules Feiffer. Published by Michael di Capua Books, an imprint of HarperCollins Publishers, Inc.

Page 27. Text and illustration from *Anansi and the Moss Covered Rock,* by Eric A. Kimmel, illustrated by Janet Stevens. Text copyright © 1988 by Eric A. Kimmel. Illustrations copyright © 1988 by Janet Stevens. Published by Holiday House, Inc.

Page 32. Text and illustration from *Froggy Gets Dressed,* by Jonathan London, illustrated by Frank Remkiewicz. Text copyright © 1992 by Jonathan London. Illustrations copyright © 1992 by Frank Remkiewicz. Used by permission of Viking Penguin, a division of Penguin Group (USA), Inc.

Page 59. Text and illustration from *Don't Let the Pigeon Drive the Bus,* by Mo Willems. Text and illustration copyright © 2003 by Mo Willems. Published by Hyperion Books for Children, a division of Disney Book Group.

Page 64. Illustration from *Minnie and Moo Go to the Moon,* the first of fifteen Minnie and Moo books by Denys Cazet. Text and illustration copyright © 1998 by Denys Cazet. Published by DK Publishing.

Page 66. Illustration from *The Cat on the Mat Is Flat,* by Andy Griffiths, illustrated by Terry Denton. Text copyright © 2006 by Backyard Stories Pty Ltd. Illustration copyright © 2006 by Terry Denton. Used by permission of Feiwel and Friends, an imprint of Macmillan Children's Publishing Group. All rights reserved.

Page 70. Text and illustration from *Fox on Wheels,* by Edward Marshall, illustrated by James Marshall. Text copyright © 1983 by Edward Marshall. Illustrations copyright © 1983 by James Marshall. Used by permission of Dial Books for Young Readers, a division of Penguin Group (USA), Inc.

Page 88. Illustration from *Matilda,* by Roald Dahl, illustrated by Quentin Blake. Text copyright © 1988 by Roald Dahl. Illustrations copyright © 1988 by Quentin Blake. Used by permission of Puffin Books, a division of Penguin Group (USA), Inc.

Page 97. Text and illustration from *Diary of a Wimpy Kid,* by Jeff Kinney. Text and illustration copyright © 2007 by Wimpy Kid, Inc. Used by permission of Amulet Books, an imprint of Harry N. Abrams, Inc., New York. All rights reserved.

Page 106. Illustration from *Junie B. Jones Has a Monster under Her Bed,* by Barbara Park, illustrated by Denise Brunkus. Text copyright ©1997 by Barbara Park. Illustrations copyright © 1997 by Denise Brunkus. Used by permission of Random House Children's Books, a division of Random House, Inc. Any third party use of this material, outside of this publication, is prohibited. Interested parties must apply directly to Random House, Inc. for permission.

Page 115. Illustration from *Knights of the Kitchen Table,* by Jon Scieszka, illustrated by Lane Smith. Text copyright © 1991 by Jon Scieszka. Illustrations copyright © 1991 by Lane Smith. Used by permission of Viking Penguin, a division of Penguin Group (USA), Inc.

Page 123. Illustration from *If You're Not Here, Please Raise Your Hand: Poems about School* by Kalli Dakos, illustrated by G. Brian Karas. Text copyright © 1990 by Kalli Dakos. Illustration copyright © 1990 by G. Brian Karas. Reprinted by permission of Simon & Schuster Books for Young Readers, an imprint of Simon & Schuster Children's Publishing Division.

Page 124. Illustration from *Laugh-eteria,* by Douglas Florian. Text and illustration copyright © 1999 by Douglas Florian. Used by permission of Harcourt Children's Books, an imprint of Houghton Mifflin Harcourt Publishing Company. All rights reserved.

Page 126. Illustration from *You Read to Me, I'll Read to You: Very Short Fairy Tales to Read Together,* by Mary Ann Hoberman, with illustrations by Michael Emberley. Text copyright © 2004 by Mary Ann Hoberman. Illustrations copyright © 2004 by Michael Emberley. Used by permission of Little, Brown and Company. All rights reserved.

Page 134. Illustration from *Babymouse: Queen of the World,* by Jennifer L. Holm and Matthew Holm. Copyright © 2005 by Jennifer L. Holm and Matthew Holm. Used by permission of Random House Children's Books, a division of Random House, Inc. Any third party use of this material, outside of this publication, is prohibited. Interested parties must apply directly to Random House, Inc. for permission.

Page 137. Illustration from *The Adventures of Ook and Gluk, Kung-Fu Cavemen from the Future,* by George Beard and Harold Hutchins. Copyright © 2010 by Dav Pilkey. Reprinted by permission of The Blue Sky Press, an imprint of Scholastic, Inc.

Index

Page numbers in **bold** refer to illustrations